Janey
The Vet

Saving Sri Lanka's
Street Dogs

JANEY LOWES

Michael O'Mara Books Limited

First published in Great Britain in 2020 by
Michael O'Mara Books Limited
9 Lion Yard
Tremadoc Road
London SW4 7NQ

A CIP catalogue record for this book is available from the British Library.

Papers used by Michael O'Mara Books Limited are natural,
recyclable products made from wood grown in sustainable
forests. The manufacturing processes conform to the
environmental regulations of the country of origin.

ISBN: 978 1 78929 199 5 in hardback print format
ISBN: 978 1 78929 200 8 in ebook format

1 2 3 4 5 6 7 8 9 10

Designed and typeset by: Claire Cater
Printed and bound by CPI Group (UK) Ltd, Croydon, CR0 4YY

www.mombooks.com

CONTENTS

To Finn, my darling boy, and all the resilient and brave lost doggies who continue to inspire me and push me forward every day. You are the reason behind everything I do and I can't thank you enough for showing me what unconditional love and true 'grit' are. And to Fred and Vinura, our too-soon departed WECare heroes, who helped save so many others with their love, compassion and dedication towards those who are ignored by so many.

PROLOGUE

I'd come in early to my vet practice in Sri Lanka, supposedly for some peace and quiet to work out what to do with Rosie, a poor pup who had come in with a serious jaw injury. Despite my best efforts, the signs weren't looking good.

It seems she had picked up food laced with explosives and was now obviously in excruciating pain. Some of the farmers in the nearby village thought this was a good way to deal with the wild boar that had been destroying their fences of late, but of course it was inevitable that other animals, including dogs, were eating the food. I had tried to patch poor Rosie up as best as I could the day before, and she was on heavy pain relief, but whether she would ever be able to eat again remained to be seen. I felt I needed to find a better way to repair her jaw, but without an X-ray machine in our makeshift clinic it was a tough ask.

I'd only just lifted Rosie onto the treatment table and started examining her for overnight developments, when Jo, the office manager of the WECare clinic, came through.

'A dog has been bitten by a crocodile and is on her way here.'

I glanced up in surprise. Once a croc got involved, survivors were rare.

'Apparently she wriggled free at an opportune moment,' Jo shrugged, 'but her sides are in bits, so the owner is on his way with her.'

If the dog was to survive, I imagined she was going to need extensive and urgent surgery. Not ideal when I desperately needed to give Rosie my full attention before the nurses arrived to run through the updates on the thirty dogs that were currently being treated in the clinic. The kennels and garden area were overflowing with pups who needed our help.

There was the blind Alsatian who had been dumped on our doorstep last night, plus the road traffic accident injuries, the amputations, the STDs (yup, dogs get them too, but more on that later!), the maggots … Sri Lanka might have a beautiful tropical climate perfect for sunbathing and exploring as a tourist, but it was also ideal for maggots, and it felt like we had them coming out of our own ears, never mind those of the dogs.

'Come look at this!' Jono, one of the clinic volunteers, shouted through. An Aussie surfer and dog lover, this job and the island's lifestyle were perfect for him.

I went through to where he had been working on physio with Timmy. The poor chap had come in after being hit by a tuk-tuk and he had not taken well to the amputation of his back leg, refusing for the last couple of weeks to even try and walk on three legs. Instead he had lain in his cage, listless, and disinterested in any interaction. I had been worrying what the future held for him.

'Stay over there and call him over,' Jono instructed.

I bent down, holding out for the slightest glimmer of an improvement. 'Come on then, Timmy my lovely!' and carried on muttering encouraging words.

Tentatively Timmy heaved his white and tan body onto

three legs and began shakily making his way towards me, one slow hop at a time.

Arriving, he promptly sat at my feet, and I couldn't stop praising him, absolutely delighted at the improvement. As he looked up at me with these big trusting eyes, that finally looked to have some life and happiness back in them, I knew Timmy was going to be okay again.

I smiled as I headed back to work out how to move forward with Rosie. Some days I wondered what had possessed me to give up my nice life in the UK five years ago and move to Sri Lanka to work with the street dogs. But moments like this one right here were my answer. Missing family and friends, constantly scraping around for money – even doing without proper chocolate and Wotsit crisps – were all worth it, if every day I could give dogs like Timmy a second chance at life.

CHAPTER ONE

FALLING IN LOVE

The first true love of my life was called Finn. As soon as I set eyes on him at sixteen years old I told my colleagues he was perfect for me, and soon he was by my side for eleven blissful years. Whether it was walking on the fell or snuggling in bed, I couldn't think of anyone else I would rather be with. And those big brown eyes … they would melt anyone's heart.

Finn was a beautiful liver brown and white spaniel, brought into the vets where I was on work experience at the time. He was unwanted at six months old by his original owner due to a potential eye issue (that was thankfully easily sorted) and became mine.

We were together as much as possible; Finn would even come along to school sometimes and sit on the side of the pitch, patiently waiting while I was playing hockey.

Whenever I did have to leave him, he would always meet me at the door carrying a shoe, or some other 'gift' to welcome me home. He was so keen to bring me these presents, he would start panicking if he couldn't find anything.

He was just perfect and while most of my family's other dogs were working dogs, kept outside in kennels, he was allowed into the house and slept in my bed with me. I'd talk to him and I swear he would understand every single word I was saying, and was in tune with exactly how I was feeling. He was like my child and best friend rolled into one.

My amazing Finny was my favourite animal growing up, but he wasn't the only one in my life. In fact, I was surrounded by animals from the start.

I grew up in Barnard Castle, a small market town in County Durham, right in the middle of really wild, beautiful countryside. You couldn't grow up there and not feel at least some connection with nature.

My dad's family were farmers, as was a close family friend, and I was always asking to be outside at their houses, exploring the land and watching the animals.

My brother was a gamekeeper and worked on some of the biggest shoots in the country. He had about ten spaniels around him at any one time, and from the age of eleven he had me out grouse beating all summer, every summer, on the fell. I loved feeling that I was somewhere very few people ever went, enjoying the remoteness and the silence – bar the sounds of birds and grasshoppers – with the dogs each side of me. I basically spent my school holidays falling in love with nature. Not the worst kind of upbringing!

When I was eleven, I sat exams to get into Barnard Castle School, an independent school with a really good reputation. I was one of five siblings and there was no way we could have afforded the fees, but Mum told me to sit the exam, which turned out to be for a scholarship, and happily I got it. Mum has always pushed me to go for my goals and opened every door for me that she could. She is really bright, but had put her own career on hold to bring up a family, so has always been really keen I make the most of every opportunity. Not that she put things on hold for ever – she went back to university as a mature student years later, and retrained as a nurse. So while I was training to help dogs, she was helping people.

When it came down to it I didn't want to go to the 'posh' school, but wanted to stay with all my mates at the local comprehensive, so Mum and I made an agreement that if I didn't like it after a year I could leave – not before that though, as she had spent so much on the school uniform! Needless to say, as soon as I got there and saw all the amazing sports facilities, the fact that the teachers were really social and relaxed, and met people who were to become lifelong friends, I told her there was no way I was leaving.

I'm so glad I made that decision to stay, as while it's a bit of a cliché, the years I spent at that school were honestly the best of my life. I was lucky enough to be captain of various sports teams, did well in lessons, and made lots of lifelong friends. Put simply, I was really happy.

Take the fact that I worked hard and was particularly interested in science and the way the body works, and combine that with my love of animals, and it is maybe a no-brainer that I wanted to be a vet for as long as I can remember. The downside to that career choice is just how many other people also want to be vets. As a result, there are a lot of prerequisites before you can even think about applying for training, including as much work experience as possible. I managed to get some at the local vet practice and fitted that in around my schoolwork. I had a great time – not least because this is the stint where I met and adopted my best buddy, Finn.

After finishing my A levels, I managed to get into Nottingham University to study Veterinary Science, which is no mean feat, when you find out that fifteen applicants were vying for each of the hundred spots.

As Mum drove me there in her car packed full of all my stuff, I was really excited about the adventure ahead, and I couldn't wait to get stuck into the course, as well as student life. But as we pulled up at my new home, I was suddenly overwhelmed with anxiety, and convinced I couldn't do it. The excitement had drained out of me and been replaced by a deep feeling of dread.

It was a precursor of what was to come, as within weeks of arriving I had been reduced to an unhappy mess. I was miserable, unable to enjoy the course, had lost ten kilograms from stress, and was crying all the time. Things got so bad that Mum came and brought me home for seven weeks while I worked out what the hell was going on. I considered pulling out of the course. If I felt like this after a few weeks, how was I going to cope with a whole five years of it? But as I started looking at other courses closer to home, I kept thinking about how much I wanted to be a vet. If I thought of my future, it was the only way I saw my life panning out – I couldn't see myself doing anything else. I also couldn't see any tangible reason why my first weeks at university had appeared to have such an impact on me.

I saw a doctor and was diagnosed with depression caused by a chemical imbalance, and put on medication. This made more sense, and no longer felt like my studies were to blame.

As the medication began working, I decided if I focused on the end goal and didn't worry too much about the day to day, maybe

I'd get through my degree. So I armed myself with all sorts of extra tactics for coping, such as a new-found love of meditation, and headed back to get my head down and concentrate on catching up. I didn't want anything to stop me getting the career I was sure I was meant to have.

In the end, university life turned out to have a lot more positives than I had expected. I developed loads of good friends, and once I had moved out of student halls from the second year onwards, I was able to have Finn living with me, which was amazing. I also enjoyed it when we got to put everything we were learning into practice on the university-owned dairy farm. Like most vet universities, there is a farm sector so you can actually learn on the animals directly, then the rest of the time it is a working farm.

At this stage if you had asked me what type of vet I was going to be, I would have been adamant I was going to work with farm animals. I guess partly because it was what I had known growing up, but also I liked the idea of working outside rather than indoors, and travelling around to different locations rather than being stuck in one clinic. So I threw my focus into that area of my studies, and even wrote my dissertation on uterine prolapse in cows. My study was published in a veterinary journal called '*Cattle Practice*' – all good preparation for having my own book one day, right?

Then finally it was time to do what I had been waiting for – apply for jobs and get stuck into being a vet for real.

I took six months out and went travelling, then got my first job in a small practice of seven staff in Alston, Cumbria. It was mixed – it dealt with farm and domestic animals – and was an hour's drive away from where I was now living in Newcastle. Alston is in the North Pennines and has been described as England's Last Wilderness. Let's just say that is an apt description, and it was a tough area to cope with working in winter. There is no way you could get out to all your visits around the farms without a 4x4 and snow tyres, and even then there was no guarantee.

I was looking forward to getting stuck into some exciting cases but, as expected when straight out of university, I was at the bottom of the pecking order. There was no chance the more exciting techniques I'd been learning about for the last five years were about to get put to use any time soon; nor would I be getting my hands on the gold standard, top-of-the range equipment. Instead my tasks mainly centred around being sent to farms where 200 cows were lined up waiting for me, all with their arses pointed in my direction …

I was generally there to check for pregnancies or to 'bleed' the cows. Pregnancy testing would be done by literally putting your hand (inside a very long glove) into the cow's bum, and feeling around to see if you could feel a calf's head. Simple, but effective.

Bleeding is no more glamorous. It is the process of lifting a cow's tail and taking a blood sample from the coccygeal vein at the base of the tail, and can be a quick way to test for diseases.

Oh, the excitement. Just what I had dreamed of doing, spending my morning working my way along the back end of 200 cows!

But I took it all as part of the training process and knew I'd have to work my way up the ladder. Sure enough, my first bigger job came when I was taking my turn on call one night. It was four a.m. in the depths of winter, and I was needed on a farm in the middle of nowhere, to deal with what turned out to be my first caesarean.

I was driving across the moor, surrounded by snowdrifts, and called my boss on the way to tell him what was happening. 'I've not done one before. Can you come?'

He jumped in his car to come and join me, but almost instantly got stuck in a snowdrift, so he rang his wife to come instead, as she was also a vet – but incredibly she got stuck in the snow too. Or at least, looking back, that is what they told me – maybe their beds were just too warm and appealing! So I had to do my first caesarean all by myself, which was stressful and full on, but I had seen a lot of them before, so I stayed calm and focused and did my best. I felt a sense of pride at the end when a sopping and wobbly calf was successfully welcomed into the world. It was a real confidence boost.

Even as the job developed in responsibility, though, it didn't feel like it was all it had been cracked up to be. Given the total stress I had gone through for five years to get there, I was feeling put out, to say the least. Surely this wasn't it? I'd pinned my hopes on this dream career at the end of all the studying, and the reality was I wasn't really bowled over.

I tried to work out if it was this specific job that I wasn't enjoying. I didn't like being on call one out of every three nights and, thanks to the location, ended up forking out for a cheap hotel on those nights, which felt like a depressing way of life. I was also questioning my choice to focus on farming. Farm vets are often limited in what they can do because the animals they deal with are looked upon differently. They are seen as part of a business, as opposed to being pets. So whereas a loving owner might be willing to fork out endless amounts of money to improve life for their pooch, if a cow is worth £200, a farmer will view it that they can only afford to spend a maximum of £200 to fix any problems. I wasn't going to be getting stuck into tendon repairs, or surgery for left displaced abomasums, any time soon (LDAs are when one of a cow's four stomachs moves into the space left after the birth of a calf). I felt lost as I had been set on farm veterinary and never considered doing small animals, but I needed a change.

There was nothing for it but to take a risk and see if things could be improved. So I took the plunge and accepted a job at a place called Westway Veterinary Group, which specialised in small animals. They are based in Newcastle and it was the exact opposite of the place I had just left.

From a team of seven, I was now in one of the biggest vet practices in the North, with around 180 staff and about 60 people in the building each day. A bonus was I was now only on call around one night a month, and three weekends a year, as opposed to twice a week.

Right from the off it was full-on work, and we were operating at a high level, but it was fun too, with music playing and people laughing and joking. I had a really full caseload to deal with, but I instantly loved it and thrived because I was being stretched. I also had a good team around me and went home feeling proud of what I had done each day, which enabled me to focus on the aspects of the job that I enjoyed.

It freed me up to see where my passions actually were within veterinary, and it soon became clear they were surgery, cardiology, and client communication. The latter is a real obsession of mine.

Traditionally, it has been a problem that lots of people going into veterinary are highly intelligent, but lack basic communication skills. Classically, vets were associated with old tweed-wearing men who would be short, sharp and cold to pet owners, and who you couldn't really speak to. Even today, I'd say 30 per cent of vets are shocking communicators, which isn't ideal for a client-facing profession, and interpersonal skills should maybe be incorporated more into veterinary teaching.

I wanted to be the exact opposite of that and am passionate about talking to people and getting to know them. I think it is part of what makes me a good vet.

I am a huge believer in having a rapport with my clients and helping them through difficult situations and celebrating with them through the good times.

I think sometimes vets get put on pedestals by the general public – and sometimes we put ourselves on pedestals – and it isn't the best way to be. We should be behaving like normal people with feelings and emotions when having conversations with a client about their pet's future. Often you are making a life-changing decision about one of their family members, so you should try and feel like part of the family.

The same goes for crying. Some vets are horrified when I have been reduced to tears in front of a client. But if I truly give a shit about that animal and the tears come, I don't really try and hide them. Is it the worst thing for an owner to see how much you care for their pet? I think not.

My methods must have been working anyhow, because just a year after I started at Westway, I was asked to open up a new branch in Wideopen.

It was a real challenge, but exciting, and gave me a whole new bunch of skills to learn on top of being a vet, and it was something to really get my teeth stuck into.

If you had asked me at that point what the next few years looked like for me, I would have said I'd probably end up as a clinical director for Westway, while living in Newcastle for the foreseeable future.

Little did I know what huge life changes were just around the corner …

· CHAPTER TWO ·

HEAVEN'S
HELLISH SIDE

Barnard Castle School Yearbook, 2007
Student voted most likely to give it all up
and become a WAG: Janey Lowes

Thanks for the vote of confidence, guys!

The reason for my nomination (I hope) was not that I was viewed as vacuous, fashion-obsessed, trophy girlfriend material. But because, as well as Finn, there was one other love of my life in my teenage years, and that was a rugby player who everyone assumed I would be with for ever, myself included.

Alex and I had started dating when I was fourteen, and he was the year above me at school. We got on so well, I fancied him like mad – he was my best friend and my soulmate in one.

It is rare for people who start dating so young to stay together in spite of everything, but we had lasted through going to different universities, through my months off travelling, and through his frequent trips away at rugby camps while he played for England. It felt like we were going to last for ever, as despite all the time apart we had always made it work. In a way, the fact we weren't in each other's pockets, but allowed each other the space to grow, felt like a real positive.

We knew each other inside out, and I only have good things to say about this amazing guy who always supported me, believed my dreams were every bit as important as his, and was never judgemental.

But things started to go downhill slowly but surely when we moved in together in Newcastle. The everyday mundaneness of our new life didn't sit well with us, even though routine is what so many people seem to crave in their relationships. I would come home tired and stressed from work, eat a ready meal, and just want to go to bed. Alex meantime was playing rugby full time and would be exhausted from a day's training or a match. It felt like those times when we were excited to see each other and it was like a real event, when we would go out for dinner or do something fun, were over. We were drifting apart and realised something was needed to shake things up if we were to salvage the relationship. So we booked what was meant to be the absolute trip of a lifetime to Sri Lanka in May 2014. Two weeks travelling the island, followed by one week staying on the south coast in a yoga and surfing retreat. Bliss.

However, it turned out that it was too late for us – we split up at the airport on the way out of Britain, before the plane had even taken off. It wasn't even really caused by an argument, but was more of a natural progression, as we both knew deep down that it was over. We pushed ahead with the holiday regardless, in a kind of weird friends/exes who get on zone.

The travelling was amazing, but the last week staying in a place called Talalla Retreat was probably the easiest, as we were hanging out with other people while surfing. It kind of took the pressure off us, and we could just relax and have a really good time. I can't say I was a good surfer at the time, but I was competent, as I had surfed as a teenager. While most people don't seem aware of it, the North East actually has quite a big surfing culture, and is probably second only to Cornwall in the UK in that respect.

It had been a great trip to Sri Lanka so far. Everywhere we went was all about beaches, sunshine, friendly locals and simple, tasty food. Each day it felt like we were waking up in paradise, with the birds chattering outside, monkeys jumping through the trees, and geckos running around the paths.

I particularly fell in love with Talalla though. A small coastal village, it is centred around the most incredible two-kilometre-long beach of golden sand, with a backdrop of palm trees and dense vegetation. There were next to no guesthouses, restaurants or bars, and the only people you tended to see on the beach were those staying at the retreat, or the local fishermen, who would head out in the night to fish, and return in the early hours to drag their boats up to shore. It was absolute heaven.

There was just one huge problem. A huge problem made up of a lot of soulful eyes staring out of mange-ridden, or injured bodies, asking for help, or with an expression on their faces that showed they had just about given up on life. The street dogs.

Wherever we were, whatever we were doing in Sri Lanka, there was guaranteed to be a street dog within sight. Sometimes they would trot over, inquisitive or friendly, and look as though life wasn't going too badly for them. But other times they would watch you from a distance, wary, but interested, and often looking in the most horrendous health. Furless with scabby, tough skin, limping, or with open sores or cuts.

The healthier-looking ones seemed to be living a pretty decent life. Roaming around as they pleased, spending their days between lying on the beach and having their pick of the scraps around the hotels. A lot of people assume the street dogs are starving and will be skin and bones, but one thing I can say is not many of them are underweight. The locals put their rubbish out to burn, but the dogs will often get in there first and help themselves to all sorts.

The odd lucky one will have made friends with locals or westerners and are particularly well fed and healthy. One who fell into this camp was Joy, a hyperactive tan-coloured two-year-old, who hung around the beach in front of Talalla Retreat, and was a favourite with the staff and holidaymakers.

She would spend the day dashing around, stopping for a rest, then off again, bouncing in circles, just excited to be hanging around with people, and getting petted by the guests. Hers was a good street dog life – one filled with food, attention, and freedom.

But there were two dogs in particular who really got under my skin on that trip.

The first one we came across on the beach. He was very typical of so many of the dogs in the country, in that he was riddled with mange. Mange is a skin condition caused by parasitic mites that is highly contagious and easily passed on between dogs. The obvious signs that a dog has it are relentless scratching, scabs and hair loss, which can be in patches, right through to a dog being completely bald. Very unoriginally, I named this new pal of mine Itchy. I really felt for him, as the irritation it was causing him was so all-consuming. There seemed to be barely a moment he wasn't scratching away to deal with one painful spot or another. I cursed myself for not having at least some antiparasitic treatment with me to help relieve his suffering a little.

Another dog I came across on the beach in Talalla was Tom, a six-year-old brown dog who had a nasty gash under his eye. He was really friendly and came over to be petted, trusting me when I wanted to take a look at his injury. It was a simple cut that I could have dealt with in no time back in the UK with a few stitches. My concern was less about the cut itself and more about what would happen next. Even with my brief knowledge of the country, I knew that untreated in a tropical climate like Sri Lanka's, it wouldn't take long for the cut to become infected and attract flies. They would come and lay their eggs in the wound, and when they hatched … *voilà*, you have an injury full of maggots. I had seen first hand what fly-strike could do to sheep and rabbits back in the UK, and was aware that the weather conditions here meant it was a real likelihood for dogs too.

I didn't have any of my veterinary equipment with me, but I didn't want to leave Tom with this injury that had potential to kill him, so I decided I would pay for him to be treated in a local clinic. Except it wasn't as simple as that. Every vet I approached told me, 'No way are we touching a street dog, you can't bring him in here.'

How was it possible that I was willing to pay for this dog's treatment but no one would look after him? Did it really matter that he lived on the street as opposed to in someone's house? Was he not the same type of animal, and was my money not the same regardless? I was shocked, as I knew in the UK we would treat any animal, if someone was willing to cover the treatment costs.

I couldn't sleep that night for thinking about Tom, and getting more and more frustrated at the simple step it would take to save his life. But other than make a promise to myself to take a basic veterinary kit with me on every future holiday, there was nothing I could do.

Sure enough, even once I flew back home, I couldn't put Tom out of my mind. There *had* to be a way to improve life for him and his canine buddies, and I was determined to work out what it was. I didn't want it to be a case of 'I am now the other side of the world, it is no longer my problem'. In fact, my mind wasn't letting that happen, whether I wanted it to or not. So I started googling to find out about animal charities in the country that helped street dogs, and thinking about any way that I could make a difference.

Could I actually go back out there for a bit, and treat these street dogs as a vet could – and should? It would be a very different experience to veterinary back home, but that would surely make me a better vet in the long run.

The limbo set-up that Alex and I had been able to exist in through our holiday had to end now we were back in the UK. It was time for me to move out of our home and decide what I was going to do next.

It would have been the easiest option to just get a new place to live and carry on with the same kind of life in Newcastle that I was already living. But I knew it would just feel like a flatter and emptier version without Alex in it, and that if I ever did want to make any big life changes, however temporary, now was the time to do it. Having no boyfriend or home was about as free as I was ever going to be from those ties that stop you doing anything too crazy or spontaneous. The split opened my eyes in a way, and made me see that now was my chance to do anything I wanted. I needed to just go for it, before I set myself up with a new set of excuses to keep from pushing boundaries.

Slowly but surely the seeds of an idea started to form. Wouldn't a change of scene be good for me for a while? I was always saying that I wanted to travel more, and everything I had in the UK could surely be put on hold for a bit …

I started seriously considering going back to Sri Lanka, this time with my own veterinary kit, and getting to work for free on these much neglected and forgotten street dogs, perhaps through one of the charities I'd found. I really wanted to give so many of them a chance at happiness they wouldn't otherwise see.

Let's face it, it wouldn't be the worst thing to live in such a beautiful country for a while, with the beach right on my doorstep …

Travelling there solo didn't concern me. After graduation and before I took my first job, I'd travelled for six months through Borneo, Bali, Australia, New Zealand and Fiji. I'd met up with friends for various sections of it along the way, but ultimately it had been my trip and I'd had the time of my life. I've always been keen to see the world, and had found travelling motivating and liberating, so wasn't worried on that front.

The main question was more, 'How could I actually make a meaningful difference to the life of the dogs if I was based out there?'

I could see there were a handful of charities scattered around the country that aimed to help the street dogs, mostly run by Europeans. My worry was that all the people who had set up these charities seemed to be well-meaning individuals as opposed to vets, and I couldn't see too much online about their set-ups, so I was a bit worried about whether my ethics and way of working would align with theirs.

I was still in the early throes of formulating a plan, but realised I needed to talk to Nick, my boss at Westway, sooner rather than later. He was like a cool, super-chilled uncle to everyone, rather than a scary boss, and was really good at managing people. He had always been super supportive in my time there, but I was worried that he might feel he had put all his faith in me the year before by putting me in charge of the new clinic opening, only for me to announce my departure. There was no way around it though – my head and my heart were already set on getting back to Sri Lanka to start treating the dogs.

As it happened, the conversation couldn't have gone any better. Nick told me he was proud of me for wanting to do something, and continued, 'I travelled when I was younger and it was the best thing I ever did. Get it out of your system, then come home in a year.

'But in the meantime, why work for another charity? Why don't you set one up yourself? I will give you ten thousand pounds from Westway to help you get started with it.'

Wow, how is that for the perfect boss!

From that point onwards Nick was great and really involved, always pushing me to do what I felt was right. So the next step for me was working out the focus of the charity. 'Help the street dogs' was too vague. How I was going to do that was the main target to work out.

The most successful organisation in Sri Lanka dealing with the street dogs seemed to be one called Embark, based in the capital, Colombo. It had been set up by a woman called Otara Gunewardene, a Sri Lankan model, who also owned a chain of stores called Odel. A bit like Debenhams, she sold them to a Japanese company a few years ago and is now hugely rich and successful. Imagine the Victoria Beckham of Sri Lanka, and you pretty much get the idea. She is also big on animal welfare and the fact she had shown so much interest in street dogs had been crucial in making changes to the thinking in the country to date. Knowing this, I got in touch with Embark to see if they had any thoughts on where I could focus my attention. All I knew was that I was keen to base myself back in Talalla. While I had only been at the retreat for a week, it felt like a starting point in terms of knowing a few people, and I had really liked the area.

Incredibly, Otara came back to me and said she would like to meet up with me, so she flew over to the UK to see our vet practice, and to have a chat. I showed her around the clinic and she told me that the most useful thing she believed a vet could tackle in the country that would really help make a difference was neutering and vaccination; vaccination to tackle a number of diseases that have been eradicated or at least controlled in many other countries, and neutering, as there were too many dogs on the island for it to cope. The poor female dogs were getting pregnant, having a litter, seeing one or two of their puppies survive beyond infancy if they were lucky, and then getting impregnated again. Her suggestions made total sense, so I decided my charity would focus its attention on that.

In the end, it was decided to call the charity WECare

Worldwide – W for Westway, and E for Embark, to reflect the support they were both giving me in getting it started.

I tied up the rest of the loose ends in my life, sold my car and told Alex about my plans. We were still close, and as always he had been super supportive of my idea. Looking back I wonder if I thought we weren't really over, and that this was a break to allow us both to do our own things, before we would then settle down together. It was hard to imagine life without him – we had been together for twelve years, nearly half my life. How would I cope without him by my side? But I was now totally free. If I didn't do it then, I would never do it, so I pushed the thoughts aside, and instead focused on packing everything I thought I would need for my new life. As well as the usual bits and pieces for myself, I put in surgical kits, bandaging, and natural products such as Manuka honey, which can help with wound management. I was worried about airline rules and what I would be allowed to bring into the country, and still had very little idea of what I would be facing, so kept it to the basics.

I booked my flight for 13 October 2014, and once I had my ticket the time just flew and suddenly it was departure day. My whole family came to the airport to see me off, like it was a day trip for them. They were all really supportive of what I was doing, and I think assumed it was the latest Janey adventure. Because I had travelled before they weren't too worried, but saw it as me moving on with my life, with the added bonus of doing something to help animals.

I have kept a photo of Tom from the day that I met him on the beach with his cut eye, and I always look back at it, and think, 'Yup, this is where it all started, buddy. It is all your fault!'

· CHAPTER THREE ·

A NEW LIFE

Looking back at the twenty-six-year-old me on that plane to Sri Lanka, I see such a different person to the one I am today. It might only be five years ago, but I seem so innocent and naive about the journey ahead. I honestly believed I was off on a kind of adventure, where I'd get the island's dogs all sorted in a year, and then be on my way to the next phase in my life. As if …

In reality I was about to embark on the most challenging, emotionally draining, and exhilarating few years of my life. The trials as well as the achievements have been insane, and let's just say I've had to do a lot of learning. To describe it as a rollercoaster ride doesn't even come close. While I wouldn't change it for the world, maybe it was better that the girl who sat on the flight that day thought it would be all plain sailing; that I would get the dogs vaccinated and neutered, manage to keep some emotional distance from them, and be back in Newcastle before I knew it. If I had known exactly what lay ahead, I might have been totally overwhelmed, and just turned around and got on the next plane back home!

As it was, I was just impatient to land in my new home, 5,000 miles away from my friends, family, and everything I had known in life so far, and get on with the challenge ahead of me. Of course I'd had some last-minute doubts about the move – the main one being about leaving Finn, my absolute best mate in the world. How could I explain to him that I was leaving him with Alex for the year so I could do this?

I was sure he would approve if he could understand, but the problem was he couldn't, and it broke my heart to think Finn might feel I had abandoned him. But I reassured myself we would have many more years together once I was back, and I could make it up to him then.

Landing in Colombo was a relief. Finally, five months after promising the poor dogs of the island that I would be back to help, I was going to get a chance to see if I could make a difference.

Grabbing my luggage and surfboard, I headed on through to the money exchange. The Sri Lankan rupee is a closed currency, meaning it isn't supposed to leave the country. Therefore you can't exchange your cash until you are in Sri Lanka, and you shouldn't leave with any significant sums of it in your possession either.

Stepping out into the heat – no cold English winter for me, thank you – I loaded my bags into a taxi and we headed south. I watched out of the window revelling in the fact that this time I wasn't looking at a holiday destination, but my new home.

If you have never been to Sri Lanka, then the best way I can describe travelling on their roads is it is an experience … Cars, buses, tuk-tuks, trucks and mopeds are all fighting it out for space; drivers oblivious to road signs or the occasional markings just seem to press their horns and hope. Overtaking happens any time and any place, regardless of whether there is actually room. Then you have to watch out for pedestrians who rarely have pavements to walk on, but meander along the roadside, suddenly stepping out to avoid haphazardly parked vehicles, sleeping dogs, or temporary sellers set up at the roadside. The resulting effect is best described as noisy, hilarious chaos.

Our route took us around the outskirts of Colombo. While you get chain stores in the city centre, as you move outwards, you are more likely to see the shops I was passing now – basic, single-room buildings selling everything from mobile phones to clothing, as well as rows of roadside shacks, shelters and stalls, filled with fresh and dried fish, and all sorts of amazing fruit and vegetables at tiny prices. There are also plenty of shops selling car parts and carrying out repairs – maybe not surprising given the road etiquette I've just mentioned.

We passed schoolchildren making their way home in their immaculate all-white uniforms, all the girls with their black hair in neat, long plaits, and the boys with their ankles poking out the bottom of the drainpipe-style trousers. The cleanliness of the uniforms is one of the mysteries of Sri Lanka that I've never yet been able to get to the bottom of. Despite the lack of washing machines, and the dusty streets, there are never grass stains or grubby cuffs on the schoolchildren's clothes. They end the day looking as pristine as they started, something that massively impresses me, but that I cannot get my head around. Answers on a postcard, please.

Finally we escaped the hustle and bustle of the city and made it onto the Southern Expressway – the only road that can feasibly be considered a motorway in the country, and links Colombo to the south. Suddenly the scenery completely changed. Now it was endless green, thanks to the palm trees, paddy fields, and dense vegetation.

Solitary bony-looking cows were scattered about, a very different breed to those I had treated back home, and each with several cattle egrets hopping around them. These birds, a little like small white herons, hang around to get the bugs that are stirred up as the cow moves around the waterlogged fields.

A dead monitor lay in the middle of the road, its large lizard body proving to be enough of a hazard that my driver had to swerve.

'Danger, Peacocks Ahead' one roadside sign announced, and sure enough I spotted several shiny blue plumes along the fence line.

The only signs of human life were the occasional women in long skirts and large-brimmed hats working through the fields, or topless men, their dusty brown skin glowing in the sun, as they chopped into the undergrowth.

Eventually the highway came to an end at Matara, and the journey slowed as we switched onto smaller roads, running through several towns and along the coastline before finally turning off down a dirt track into Talalla Beach, and my home for the foreseeable future.

I had got on well with a few of the surf instructors at Talalla Retreat, and they had agreed to let me stay with them in The Jungle House, while I found my feet.

It was a strange feeling, waking up that first morning, thanks to the incredible dawn chorus of birds, from tuneful exotic songbirds, to squawking peacocks and parrots. I was excited, nervous, happy and sad, all at the same time. The weather and the proximity of the beach meant there was a bit of a holiday vibe, but I also had plenty of memories of being here the previous time, and was acutely aware that I was on this next phase of my life on my own. For twelve years I'd had Alex there as my rock, as someone to lean on, tell me if I was being an idiot or doing the right thing, to cheer me up and celebrate the successes with. So to wake up to do all this stuff without him was hard and weird. But I set all that to one side, as I knew if I could get through it,

I'd be a stronger person by the end. If anything, it made me more determined to get this right.

So I focused on the positive – that I was ready and raring to get started in my new role. This had been months in the planning, and I had all sorts of ideas that I wanted to get moving on. There was all this potential there in front of me to make a difference, and I was my own boss, free to work the way that made the most sense to me and keeping the hours I liked. I couldn't wait to get stuck in.

Looking back, part of me wishes I had taken some time out when I first arrived to enjoy Sri Lanka, do lots of surfing and yoga, and to travel around a bit; actually get to enjoy the country before I started working. I would soon realise that time out, once I had begun, was not going to be an option.

At the same time, I'm not too good at relaxing when I am on a mission. I've always been quite obsessive about my goals. Whether it was GCSEs, A levels, my degree, or the right job, I've always had my eye on the next target, and I think I'd be lost without something to aim for.

So that was that. From day one, I would wake up each morning and get going straight away. I'd set up with my laptop in a shady spot and get started on the day's goals. I am the biggest to-do list writer – you should see the length of some of them – and each day I would merrily crack on with ticking them off.

My initial plan was to spend a couple of days a week working on getting WECare off the ground, a couple of days volunteering at one of the other charities, and a couple of days doing some form of work to earn money to keep me going. Which left one day off for me each week. Well, it wasn't long until that all went to shit! Within weeks of arriving I was all about WECare, seven days a week, every waking hour.

I did try and do a few days' work at another charity, but in reality I didn't enjoy it, and found the set-up wasn't for me. The fact it wasn't run by vets made it tricky, as I was being given treatment plans for the dogs by someone who wasn't qualified. The part of me that had spent so long training as a vet felt protective of my profession. I am passionate about it, I worked bloody hard for it, and it is a skill that shouldn't be underestimated. So to be told by someone who wasn't trained not to give pain relief where I deemed it necessary, or to leave a wound open that I knew needed closed, was pretty painful for me.

This is not meant as a criticism of any of the other charities on the island, as the fact they even exist is awesome. To put it in perspective, there are believed to be around 30,000 animal charities in the UK, compared to six registered NGOs working with animals across Sri Lanka, so the fact that anyone has gone to the effort of starting one is amazing, it just happens that this particular one wasn't right for me. But we are all there with the same end goal – happier lives for the dogs – so whatever they are doing is more than what 99 per cent of the rest of the society is doing, and for that I take my hat off to each and every one of them.

So, then, theoretically I was entirely focused on getting the charity set up, and the neutering and vaccinations programme under way. I was being strategic and addressing the overpopulation issue, looking at improving the bigger picture. Yeah right. I hadn't considered how seeing the individual animals was going to make me feel once I was there, so it took no time at all for that focus to fall by the wayside – five days to be precise! Because as soon as I saw an unwell dog there was no way I was going to do anything other than give it my full attention and get it treated.

My very first patient turned out to be one of my doggy pals from my holiday – Joy. I loved her cheeky personality, even if she did sometimes get in trouble for jumping up at the tables in the restaurant.

Since my return I'd seen her most days, but one morning I noticed she had a wound on her head, about the size of a fifty-pence piece, that looked like it might have been caused by a bite from fighting with another dog. But rather than healing up, I could see it now had several fat, white maggots wriggling around in it.

Back in the UK in my job I had come across fly-strike – or myiasis, as it is also called – in only two types of animals: rabbits and sheep. In rabbits it is just horrible. Flies are attracted to the groin area of an animal that hasn't cleaned itself properly, they lay their eggs in its fur, and within hours maggots are hatching and starting to eat into the flesh. Often owners don't realise what is happening until it is too late, so the only course of action is to put their pet to sleep.

With sheep, farmers tend to keep a close eye as they know soiled or damp wool is an ideal place for flies to lay their eggs, and there are all sorts of sprays and products on the market to help deal with it if there is even the slightest concern.

But I had never seen a single case of maggots in a dog, so looking at this open wound with these wiggly little critters crawling around in it was quite a shock. There was nothing for it but to find a pair of tweezers and see what I could get out.

I grabbed my gear and caught up with Joy in the car park. Calling her over, I decided the best way was sedation, as I thought pulling out maggots would be horribly painful for her. It was getting dark, so I had a head torch on to help me, and soon I had cleaned the wound out as best as I could and was able to put a dressing on. Then off Joy trotted with a bandage around her head – probably not a sight that the locals had ever seen before!

After that I would do dressing changes every day, and soon enough Joy was all healed up and bouncing around the place, as crazy as ever.

I grinned to myself, happy I had already made a difference to Joy's life – although aware of just how much of a tiny drop in the ocean it was of the overall problem.

Meanwhile, the work to create WECare was a million times harder than I expected. I don't think anyone setting up a charity anticipates how difficult it will be. While I get that you can't have people setting up a charity right, left and centre with the click of a button, it was harder to set that thing up than to pass my vet exams! It was so tough. And that was just the paperwork for the UK – it was a whole other matter in Sri Lanka. It turned out that while WECare could be deemed a charity back home, in Sri Lanka only the temples are granted charitable status. Instead I needed to apply to be a non-governmental organisation – an NGO.

I was also trying to learn how to do everything else myself around the creation of a charity to save on costs. Tasks such as how to build a website, make banners and posters, get products in from the UK, the legal side of things … the real back room stuff that I hadn't dealt with before. Don't get me wrong, I came out of those early days with a lot more useful skills than I went in with, but it was so much stuff that I hadn't envisaged I'd need to do. At times I got really frustrated with all the paperwork – all I wanted to do was help the dogs.

So I was constantly busy, which in a way worked for me. I put my head down, and just ploughed, ploughed, ploughed. There was no way I was letting this be anything other than a total success.

• CHAPTER FOUR •

MY FIRST PATIENTS

I had looked for both of my holiday dogs, Tom and Itchy, on my return. It would have been a great feeling to have treated them – or, even better, spotted them chilling on the beach, loving life. Unfortunately, neither of them ever appeared again, and while I fear the worst, I can only hope that they had moved on elsewhere while I was back in the UK.

Once I had treated Joy, I was obviously on the lookout for my next patient, and that turned out to be Ralphie. Ahhh, my little Ralphie! It was his mum Fifi who I spotted first, as I noticed her entropion eyelids, the same condition that Finn had been suffering when we first met. Because hers had never been treated, both of her eyes had developed ulcers. I'd decided to try and sort those out, and knew she lived in an area of ground just one road back from the beach.

But when I got near her patch, I was hit by this really horrible, rotten smell. I looked under a piece of asbestos that seemed to be the source of it and was shocked to spot four puppies. Fifi had built a kind of den for them, but unfortunately two of them were already dead, and another looked like he was on his way out. Scooping out the tiny, sickly, dusky grey bundle of fur, who looked to be barely three weeks old, I could see a small wound on his neck with a few maggots crawling around. It was at the exact point where a mamma dog picks up her pups, so unfortunately I think she must have nicked his skin, and – as I was quickly learning – that is all it took for the flies to rock up and lay, and maggots appear.

The two who had died had sadly already succumbed to their maggot wounds, and that was unfortunately the cause of the awful smell.

The other puppy looked okay, so I left her where she was with her mum, and took the little bundle that I then named Ralphie back to the retreat for treatment, trying to reassure Fifi that I was doing a good thing. It is times like this when I love the innocence and instinctive trust in a dog. Somehow she knew that I was trying to help, and she accepted it.

My housemates were horrified when I arrived back with this strong-smelling, maggoty little waif and one of them said I couldn't keep him there.

'It won't be for long as unfortunately I don't think he will be alive in twenty-four hours,' I answered sadly, 'but I have to try.'

Clearly – and thankfully – I was still to learn about the resilience of the street dogs. I kept cleaning out the wound until I was able to close it up, then in no time at all Ralphie was as right as rain. Unfortunately in the meantime I had gone back to check on the fourth puppy and she had died. I felt awful that I hadn't taken her too, but at least I was able to reintroduce Ralphie to Fifi and reunite them.

Aware that the survival rate of puppies wasn't the best, and not too convinced by Fifi's parenting skills, I thought it would be better for Ralphie's chance of survival if he carried on staying with me so he had someone to look out for him. I put a collar on to him – the clearest sign in Sri Lanka that a dog is actually owned, rather than a street dog – and he became the first of my Sri Lankan dogs. Sorry, housemates, the twenty-four hours was about to become a lot longer than that.

I was desperately missing Finn though and, while no dog was ever going to fill his shoes (paws?), having the bundle of energy that was Ralphie, bounding over for regular cuddles, took the edge off for me a bit.

But when he was just twelve weeks old, Ralphie went missing. I was absolutely frantic, asking everywhere if anyone had seen him. Suddenly someone came forward to say they had spotted him being taken on a scooter. Ralphie had been stolen!

I was devastated and set a reward of 20,000 rupees for his return – around £100. I made a massive six-foot banner, offering the reward, and hung it up across the main road in the village. I am sure if the locals didn't already think I was batshit crazy before then, they did now, especially as what I was offering was about the average monthly salary in the area, but I just wanted my dog back. I'd come from a world where Finn was my everything, and there was no question I would have done that and more for him, so this seemed to be the right thing to do for Ralphie.

Whether because of the money offered, or because they wanted to keep the crazy western lady happy, the whole village began hunting for him, and eventually someone found out that it was a builder who had been working on the retreat who had taken him. He had taken Ralphie all the way to Galle – around sixty kilometres away. The locals contacted him and he was told to not ever set foot back in Talalla, which meant he couldn't come back there to work. I went to meet him to collect Ralphie. He apologised, claiming he hadn't realised he was owned, but I wasn't convinced, and was sure he had known what he was doing. While I was surprised at the strength of the local support, I was also touched at the villagers being so protective of me. After that Ralphie roamed around the village – and for miles beyond – like he was a little prince. He is a proper cheeky dog who can be a real menace, but that was it, there was no way he wasn't going to have a lot of people looking out for him for the rest of his life. But from then on everyone from the residents through to the local police knew him as Ralphie, the 20,000 rupee dog!

I had one other patient during my first fortnight in the country. I was on my way to the highway, when I spotted this super-cute dog walking with one leg that was more like a stump. It looked like his foot had been run over by a car and effectively traumatically amputated, leaving him with no toes, and this stump that would evidently have been worsening the more he used it.

He was in a really bad way, but newly named Boris wouldn't let me close enough to catch him. I was really aware of all the vehicles flying past us, so the last thing I wanted to do was scare him into the road.

I was desperate to get him the treatment he needed, so asked some dog catchers from Embark to come down from Colombo and collect him. They made the journey down, which was really good of them, and we went back to the area where I had spotted him, and sure enough he was there again, his leg looking even worse this time.

We asked around nearby homes to see if he belonged to anyone, and everyone said no, so the dog catchers scooped him up and took him off to a vet in Colombo for me.

As I'd expected, Boris's leg couldn't be saved and had to be amputated, so I agreed to pay the vet bill for it. When he had recovered, I rented a car and went to pick him up from Colombo.

He got so excited as we were travelling along that he was jumping all over the place, and pissed everywhere in the car … not my finest hour. But we finally made it back to the area where I had found Boris, and I let him out of the car, hoping he would be able to pick up on the life he had been living there before. Just as I was watching him sniff around to see what had gone on in his territory in his absence, a family came running out of a nearby wooden shack, screaming with happiness.

Luckily someone local was able to translate as they couldn't speak any English, and it turned out that he was their dog. They lived by a creek and when he had disappeared they thought he had been taken by a crocodile.

They stood smiling and kept patting him on the top of his head, which I had already learnt was a real sign of affection there. People just don't scoop up their dogs and smother them in kisses as they might do elsewhere to celebrate a return. But this small gesture of a constant head pat showed me just how much he meant to them.

I wasn't sure what they would make of their now three-limbed dog, but it turned out they had taken him to a vet about his foot previously, but had been told treatment would cost 6,000 rupees (around £30), which was way beyond their means. I was pleased they had even thought to try though, and they were happy he had been sorted and was no longer in pain. It was my first proper introduction to a Sri Lankan family who owned and really cared about their dog, and it was a lovely starting point. We have stayed in touch ever since as I call in on them and check on them and Boris whenever I am in the area.

Also in that very hectic first month, I came across some other pups who had been born on Talalla beach. They seemed to be doing okay at first, and one in particular, Lottie, was very fond of Ralphie. I used to joke that he was her girlfriend when they bounded over to play together.

Then one day I noticed a tiny wound on her leg. I was pleased, as spotting it that early on I knew I would be able to fix it easily, and prevent the dreaded maggots. All I needed was to have her at home with me for a few days and I was sure Ralphie wasn't going to object.

But within hours I noticed she was twitching and her breathing was a bit odd. A couple of days later she had a seizure and blood came from her mouth. It was so distressing, but I managed to get it under control and bring her back round. I realised she must be suffering from canine distemper and was already at the neurological stage.

Distemper is a really horrible viral disease in dogs that unfortunately has no cure at the moment. You can only try and control it through tactics such as antibiotics and administering fluids, then hope for the best. Distemper is related to measles and mumps but doesn't affect humans.

What is particularly frustrating is that it is completely preventable if the dog has been vaccinated, which is why the disease has been wiped out in the UK. It was common here in the 1970s, but then we eradicated it thanks to vaccination.

It doesn't help that it can present in many ways, so it is hard to detect and catch early. Often an animal will present a first round of symptoms, but it might be something like diarrhoea, which can be a sign of a whole host of other things. Then it clears up, but suddenly a couple of weeks or months later you are faced with full-on neurological problems, almost like seizures, and twitches. They don't normally die from it, but will get secondary infections such as pneumonia that kills them. It is the most painful death, with their whole bodies twitching and hurting.

It is why I am so keen to vaccinate as many dogs in Sri Lanka as possible for it, but the problem is, unlike rabies, where it is one jab and you are done, with distemper, you vaccinate the dog once, then need them in for a second jab two to four weeks later, and then every year after that. It's not easy to keep up to speed on the vaccinations of street dogs, but that doesn't mean I am not giving it my best shot.

In terms of Lottie, unfortunately the survival rate by the time they have reached the stage she was at is 11 per cent. But incredibly, she turned out to be a proper little trouper, and fought on through it and survived.

It didn't feel right to put her back onto the beach to fend for herself again, so she became the second of my dogs, along with Ralphie. Being honest I would say she probably suffered some brain damage as part of the distemper. During the seizure her brain would have been briefly starved of oxygen and, as with humans, this can cause some longer-term behavioural changes, but Lottie is all the more lovely and special for it.

• CHAPTER FIVE •

A FELLOW DOG WHISPERER

'd accepted that WECare was pretty much going to be just me working alone for the time being, apart from during the neutering and vaccination programme. I knew it would be pretty lonely at times, and that the language barrier was probably going to cause me its fair share of problems, but so be it.

But then, an absolute angel of a guy happened to land in my path.

At the start of November, I received an email from a lady at Embark, asking me to look into some dogs in need that were much closer to me than their headquarters.

Someone has been in touch about some dogs that are in a bit of a state, and need some help, she wrote. *Can you go and take a look?*

Absolutely, I fired back, pleased that they were thinking of me when a situation like this occurred.

Checking the location – a village about ten minutes along

the coast called Kalukatiya Watta – I gathered up my basic equipment and headed out. I flagged down a nearby tuk-tuk and held on as we bumped along the rough, dusty roads. I was nervous as I had no real idea what to expect from what was effectively my first call out.

We got to the address I'd been given and it turned out to be a building site – but what a building site. Once completed, it was clear that the ANI Villas, as they were called, were going to be a luxury five-star resort, with the most incredible clear view out to the blue sea beyond.

A worker came over and introduced himself as Malaka. He was a slim, very slight local in his late twenties, and explained shyly that it was he who had contacted the charity. Even setting aside the fact he had taken the effort to report animals in need, I warmed to him.

He took me on through the half-built walls and showed me the first dog, who the builders had named Barbie, and I gasped. The poor pup didn't have one single scrap of fur on her. She was so riddled with mange that not a single hair was poking through her cracked skin.

Luckily mange is not something you come across too often in the UK. It is a horrible condition that leaves the dog agonisingly itchy, needing to scratch 24/7. Not only that, but the scratching can open up the skin to risk of infection, making life even more miserable for any of its unfortunate sufferers.

Barbie really did look awful, and stood looking at me cautiously through big doleful eyes. I was quickly learning that when a dog has mange, no local wants to touch them or even go near them, so they are even more likely than other street dogs to get a harsh word or something thrown at them. Barbie had clearly learnt that people weren't generally there to be kind or help her, so kept a bit of a distance at first.

But like 99 per cent of dogs when faced with some kind words and treats, she began to come around, and eventually let me bathe her, using a hose pipe from the site and medication to help soothe her skin and treat the bacterial and yeast components.

Once that physical contact had been made and I kept speaking to her softly, she could see I meant it kindly, and I was looking at her with only sympathy in my eyes, she visibly relaxed.

The other builders all stood around watching me, glad of the excuse to down tools for a bit and be entertained, but they were clearly thinking I was some kind of crazy woman. As far as they were concerned, by touching Barbie, I was also going to end up with mange. (Possible, but unlikely, as the mites that cause mange in dogs are species specific, so if they pass to a human they can't breed on us, so die out.)

But it had been so ingrained in them from childhood that these street dogs were vermin and would bite or infect you, that on the whole they kept away. Their reaction to the dogs was more akin to how rats might get treated in the UK. The odd person might feed them or show them some kindness, but they are generally avoided out of fear.

They stood muttering in astonishment among themselves, and I felt myself redden with embarrassment, but tried to tune them out and focus on the job at hand. The worst thing though was the occasional outbreak of laughter. What was so funny about the state of this poor creature?

They weren't trying to be mean, and did make attempts to help, they just didn't know how to, apart from Malaka. He had a very gentle way with the dogs, and tried to assist where he could, coaxing the dogs over, and holding things as I asked him to.

A second dog on the site was called Bula, and he needed some attention too for a wound on his paw. He was a big, confident, sturdy dog, so the builders had a bit more respect for him, realising that he could act as an unofficial guard dog for the site. They had been feeding him and taken him under their wing a bit, so he was in a reasonable enough state and happy enough with humans, so I was able to patch up his wound with ease.

Then there was a third dog who Malaka pointed out, who kept scratching at his ear. As I watched him I realised it was crawling with maggots. I'd never seen anything like it through my training and career, and the size of them made Joy's few look like little babies. This unfortunate dog must be driven crazy by it, and who knew how deeply they had burrowed.

The strange thing is, at first these maggots can prove themselves to be quite useful. They eat away the dead skin, so can act like a disinfectant and stimulate the skin to start healing, but the problem is they don't know when to stop. The greedy little critters just keep going. And going … Once they are through the dead skin, they will carry on to the live stuff, and they won't stop unless they are forced to. So taking a deep breath, I realised the only thing to do was sedate my new friend and clean them out, one by one. Glancing round as the builders looked on, I spotted one of their work benches, and decided to commandeer that and carry out surgery bang in the middle of this amazing (if unfinished) villa! Hoisting my patient on to the table with the help of Malaka – who had been hovering nearby watching with interest – I got started.

Once he was sedated, I pulled on some surgical gloves, grabbed a pair of tweezers and began pulling the maggots out one by one, and dropping them into a bowl of surgical spirit to kill them.

They were fat wrigglers, and with them came plenty of pus and a bad smell. This is not a book to read while eating your dinner …

A couple of times I looked up, when deep in the work of extracting yet another maggot, to swap that horrific sight for one of the most amazing views out to the blue of the sea and the sky beyond. How could one of the most beautiful places on earth also see man's supposed best friend going through so much suffering?

I pulled out as many maggots as I could, but some of them were in too deep, and I would have risked damaging the dog's ear if I were to probe further. So I applied a powder that would kill off any remaining maggots or force them out. Then I dressed the area and bandaged it, hoping it would now get a chance to heal.

The call-out was another part of the surreal introduction to my new life, but kind of summed up the mix of highs and lows that I'd already seen on the island. It was also just one of many weird and wonderful situations I was to find myself in over the next four years.

Over the following weeks I had to go back to Bula to treat other small wounds, as he was always getting himself into scrapes, although nothing too serious. And Barbie's treatment was an ongoing task. But in no time at all she looked great and her fur grew back, making her identifiable as a typical Sri Lanka street dog.

The irony is I had been horrified at the state of her mange and thought she was in an awful way. What I hadn't yet realised was that I was to see about another 2,000 in similar mangey states over the next few years.

On my following visits, Malaka opened up about his love of dogs and the collection of animals he had amassed back at his family home in Kandy, a city in the middle of the hills, in the centre of the country. It was clear he was a very compassionate person, and quite rare in the huge amounts of empathy he had for dogs. He also spoke better English than anyone I had come across in the country so far. So when he asked if he could come and volunteer with me, I couldn't believe my luck and jumped at the chance.

Although Malaka worked a six-day week at the building site, on the seventh day he would come and join me, and we went on the hunt for dogs in need. I loved that he had only one day off a week, and yet he genuinely wanted to spend it with me, rescuing dogs. As I thought he would, he proved to be a real asset, with an inspiring work ethic, positive attitude, and dog whispering skills!

It was only as time progressed that I realised just how unique

Malaka is and how him falling into my path made things that bit more manageable. When much of the rest of the island wouldn't go near a street dog out of fear or disgust, he would be there cuddling them, loving them, and doing anything to help make their lives better. Not only that, he was choosing to do it all voluntarily, despite not being particularly financially well-off. He is the only Sri Lankan who has ever volunteered with WECare, which just speaks volumes to me about the kind of person that he is.

He has a heart of gold, and really improved the experience for me from then on. I couldn't wait for his day off each week, as I enjoyed the work that bit more. I was so thankful that I felt that I wasn't alone in this, but had someone like him at my side.

• CHAPTER SIX •

COMBING THE STREETS IN A TUK-TUK

The next few months passed in a bit of a blur.

I was spending a fair bit of time on the computer, trawling through paperwork, applying for grants, sharing information about WECare on social media, and trying to get as much donated medication as possible, so that I could eek out the £10,000 for that bit longer. Basically all the boring but crucial tasks.

I was now also treating a lot more dogs and beginning to feel I was certainly making inroads with the pooches of Talalla. There was much less chance of coming across a dog with an untreated wound or broken limb, and their skin was looking much better.

I also moved out of The Jungle House and into my own place. It had been great living with the guys, but I needed my own space, and I think they were getting sick of all my inpatients!

My new pad was a three-bedroom, single-storey house, just along from the retreat, and still in Talalla village, just one road back from the beach. My rent was 65,000rupees (£300) a month, and crucially it had a secure garden – rare in Sri Lanka but super necessary for the dogs. I still had Ralphie and Lottie, as well as two sisters called Lilo and Stitch who were living with me long term, and then generally another half-dozen others staying with me while they recuperated.

Malaka kept saying how much he enjoyed the work, and I was realising just how badly I needed a full-time assistant. So I did the maths and offered him a wage to come and join me full time from May 2015. I was really excited about this as I knew how good he was, but also it made it feel like it was becoming a team effort. I wasn't just dealing with this all on my own, but had someone whose full-time job it was to make WECare work as well. From that moment onwards he was my right-hand man, and we did everything together.

We fell into a bit of a routine – or at least as much of a routine as you can get in life in Sri Lanka.

I would be woken most mornings by the trilling sounds made by Indian palm squirrels – really hyper, striped chipmunk-esque creatures – then start the day dealing with inpatients at my house, and any computer admin work. Meantime Malaka would be putting out feelers about dogs in need. Sometimes he would have heard about one from a friend or through village chat, or other times he would go to nearby villages and chat to the locals about any they had seen. Then he would come and get me to do the vet part.

Other times we would drive around in a tuk-tuk until we spotted a dog who needed our help – which sadly never took long – then I would treat them at the roadside, while Malaka assisted me.

The main injuries we were dealing with were caused by road traffic accidents, fights with other dogs, and mistreatment by humans, with many of the injuries inflicted providing a home for the dreaded maggots. Then there was the bad skin, the ticks and the lice.

That very first maggot wound I dealt with on Joy, and thought was massive, was the size of a fifty-pence piece … well, it didn't take long until that seemed like nothing. I'd seen wounds as big as dinner plates, and no longer sedated every dog to remove the horrible wrigglers. Because the skin around the area was often dead, it didn't cause the dog as much pain as it might have and, combine that with the problems of sedating at the roadside and the resilience that these dogs have, I was quickly learning that it didn't always make sense.

As we didn't have a surgery, I was carrying out as much of the work as possible at the point where we found the dog, or in the house or garden of any kind-hearted souls who supported what we were doing, or who looked out for that specific dog.

My medical bag had been steadily growing, although it wasn't easy to get a lot of the equipment I was after, and it was proving to be more expensive than I'd anticipated. Thankfully a friend had been over to visit and brought me a bunch of supplies, so I was a bit more prepared for various scenarios, but I was definitely getting better at improvising with my use of equipment.

This is where Malaka was brilliant. He had a really creative mind in how to get around things and find replacements to do the job. So, say I needed a splint for a broken leg, he would reappear with a bit of gutter pipe that would do the job just as well. Granted, they were not as comfy as those from the UK that have padding inside, but until we were able to afford those, or if we were caught out in an emergency, this piping worked just fine.

If we were caught short without a muzzle, Malaka would make them out of bandages, by creating loops that would go around the dog's jaw and tie behind their head. They were slightly harder to get on the dog, but once they were in place worked perfectly well, and allowed us to push on with treating the dog.

When it came to actually getting close to each patient, it was a case of being resourceful, and adapting our techniques to the dog. Sometimes it was a matter of sitting and waiting for them to come to you, at other times it was about distracting them. If they were aggressive or flighty, it was about taking any opportunity that arose, and just grabbing their neck and hoping you had a proper hold of them before they could bite.

Mostly I preferred finding ways to gain their affection and trust.

Again, Malaka was the perfect right-hand man in this, as he saw the best approach in a very similar way to me. He was a natural at dealing with the dogs, and had a real affinity with them. He would take the time to just sit and reassure them, and let them come to him in their own time, rather than rushing in or trying to be bolshy or dominate.

More often than not, reassuring, comforting words, combined with the temptation of food, would eventually work, although you could never be sure what food was going to be the deal breaker.

Once in a nearby village we spotted a white dog with awful skin and a bad limp. Badger, as we named him, wouldn't let us close enough to see too much, but I didn't like the look of his paw one bit. It looked bloody, angry, infected and horribly sore.

He was particularly distrustful of humans, and would run off, or duck away if I got remotely near him. The usual tricks weren't working, and I was running out of different treats to try on him. Eventually, in desperation, I bought some buns from the local bakery and began sending little bits of them his way. Suddenly his nose started twitching and he edged closer, gobbling the pieces down. Bingo. Who knew buns were going to be the way to this boy's heart.

Finally getting him close enough to have a look, I realised poor Badger had an actual hole in his foot that was infected and, of course, filled with maggots. The poor boy had become so desperate from the pain of it that he had begun attempts to gnaw his own foot off. Luckily we had got to him just in time and were able to kill and remove the maggots, pack the wound with Manuka honey, and put a dressing on it. We saved his foot, and got him back out onto the street and to his patch within the week.

Whenever I pass that bakery I think of him, and it acts as a great reminder that whenever you think you have exhausted all the options, there is always one more – buns!

It was inevitable that everything we were doing would attract people over for a good old nose. I could be sat in the dusty road patching up a suspected fracture, and have as many as thirty people all crowded round watching what I was doing, even filming it on their phones. It was off-putting at first, but I soon got used to it, and would tune them out, and focus on the task at hand.

The other thing people did when gathered around, and that I found much harder to get used to, was laugh. What the hell is so funny about an injured dog, and my attempts to help? In the beginning it annoyed me, and made me feel embarrassed and flustered, but over time I learnt that this isn't ridiculing or mocking laughter. Many Sri Lankans actually laugh when nervous or uncomfortable, and because they weren't sure if I should be touching these dogs they were quite on edge. They were worried that I was going to get bitten, or diseased, or catch rabies, and they didn't understand why I was putting myself at risk.

They were trying to understand why this crazy woman in her flip-flops and summer dress had just chased an injured dog down the street, managed to coax it to safety, injected it, and was now covered in blood while attempting to bandage it – and didn't give a shit!

Not only were the locals not used to seeing someone handle street dogs, but I was a white female vet who was doing it. And the majority of the white people they had come across before were probably in the country to lie on the beach in a bikini. It's a sweeping statement – I know there were NGOs here after the tsunami – but the reality is most white faces will belong to tourists here to enjoy themselves as opposed to helping out or doing a job, so it added to the shock element. No one needed to explain that to me, I could see it in their faces.

But while many of the villagers didn't fully understand it, the more they saw what I was doing, the more I slowly began to gain respect. If a group of ten guys were too afraid to go near the dog earlier in the day, and I walked over by myself and was able to connect with it, it made people think. And even if they thought I was crazy, they could see I was there to do a job, and was going to do anything I needed to help that animal. Word got around quickly in every village we went to, and soon my name was never just Janey, but was always 'Dr Janey'.

I soon realised that while people wouldn't want to deal with these dogs themselves, they were thankful that someone was doing it. People are wrong when they think Sri Lankans don't care about the dogs. The majority of them absolutely do, they just don't have the means to do anything about it. No one in their right mind wants to see an animal suffer, but there just hasn't been a way to help them previously, as no vets would see them.

Compare it to driving past a badger on a road in the UK. If it was dead, you might give it a glance, and think 'what a shame', but there is practically zero chance you are going to stop and move its body or bury it.

Then imagine the badger is injured. You wouldn't know how to get near it in the first place, or how to treat it even if you could. What if the RSPCA or your local wildlife sanctuary didn't exist for you to call out?

The reality is you would probably give the badger a brief 'poor thing' glance, then go on with your day, because it was all you could think to do. That is how it has been for most Sri Lankans throughout their lives. As they don't want to see the dog badly hurt as they can't fix it, they would rather ignore it. For many of them it has been like self-preservation before now, I suppose.

Once I'd gained their trust, some of the more confident and supportive people could be brought on board to keep an eye on the welfare of the dog. We soon built up a network of villagers who were dog friendly and willing to help out. So say I had put a bandage on a dog and was aiming to come back in three days to check it, clean the wound or change the bandage, whatever was needed, there was generally someone watching who I could ask to check the dog in the meantime. They didn't need to do anything, other than contact us if something didn't seem right with the dog, or if they needed support of some kind, and to keep a lookout that the patient was around and had not moved on. In reality, 99 per cent of the time, bandage a dog, go back in three days, and they will be in exactly the same place as they were before. The streets are their territories, and a tiny section of that will be their specific home. Like humans, they stick close to home.

Malaka often acted as a translator between me and these guys, which proved invaluable. He was always so careful to make sure that both I and any person involved were completely clear on the situation, despite any language barriers.

I tried to spend time with the locals when I was in an area so that they could see I wasn't just this anonymous, aloof figure. I wanted to be as personable as I had tried to be with my clients back in the UK, so that they understood this all came from a place of caring. I also hoped it would make them more likely to contact me if there was a problem with a dog. I'd stop for a cup of tea and a chat and it would set me and the charity up well. I'd see people four years on from stopping for a cuppa after helping a dog, and we'd still remember each other.

And to be honest it's not just about the practical use of it, I enjoyed that side as well. It was almost like I was getting the bits I had liked out of both the farm and small animal vet practices back in the UK. So I was dealing with dogs, but able to get out and see people on the road, really meet the community.

I thought it would be useful to build up a bit of a network among the Western expats too, as I thought they would be animal lovers, and with no language barrier they could be useful sources of info on the dogs. But when I first arrived in Talalla, there weren't that many Brits who had actually set up home in the area. The tourism boom was still to come.

Some of those who were already there, including the guys at the retreat, were great at contacting me from the off, while others who had been there for ten-plus years had built up an immunity to what they saw, so no longer gave it too much thought.

What they were keen for, though, was a western vet for their own pets. But while I would never turn down anything where an animal might genuinely be suffering, I couldn't suddenly start travelling the country to take a look at these owned pets with smaller issues. There were local clinics the owners could turn to for that, and it would detract from the dogs who really needed me.

While word was spreading, and people were beginning to realise that I would help dogs, they still didn't fully understand in what way, or if they would get charged or in trouble, and how much responsibility they had to take for that animal etc., so there was still a lot of distrust about and I was really trying to work on that.

One morning I woke up to find a little bald puppy dumped on the doorstep of my new home. I was glad that at least someone had thought to do that, as opposed to leaving him to fend for himself, or getting rid of him in some other way. I named the little mangey pup Benji and started him on his treatment. I had intended to rehome him, but in those days I wasn't inundated with dogs, and before I knew it his sweet little personality had got under my skin, I was super attached to him, and he had become a permanent resident Chez Janey.

It was lucky I was now in my own home, as the number of dogs in my care was growing by the day. Soon after I got Benji, a friend called me, really distressed. 'Janey, I've hit a dog. I don't know what damage I've done though as I can't find her. Please help!'

He was miles away in the middle of nowhere, but there was no way I couldn't give it my best shot. For an hour we hunted the area all around the road, and eventually we found the puppy, who was to be known as Tilly from then on. Despite having a broken pelvis and two broken legs, she had managed to drag herself off the road, a hundred metres down this ravine, and up the other side, where she was hiding, until a little squeak gave her away – and saved her life.

I got Tilly back to the house and began the long process of fixing her up, much to the relief of my friend, and all in the unusual setting of my home. Creativity was becoming a natural part of the way I had to work. I used one of the bedrooms as a sort of operating theatre. There wasn't anything in it to be honest, it was more about keeping a clear and sterile space in which I could work. There is a photo of Tilly hooked up to a drip in the garden. I didn't have anywhere to hang it, so I hung the drip equipment over my bike. Make use of everything you have, and all that!

It was a long recovery for her, but she did really well, and it was lovely for her and Benji to be pups together at the house. They are the nicest dogs and the best of friends, and she is so well behaved and easy, that yes, you guessed it, Tilly ended up staying with me for the long term too, and is still with me as I write this.

What was funny is that despite the bad start her legs had in life, they became super strong and she is like a kangaroo. There was one funny day when Benji took a running jump to try and cross a river, totally missed and ended up with his face planted in the water. Tilly looked on in disgust, walked up to the river, and *boing!* From a standing start, she landed cleanly on the other side. The pair of them crack me up.

The only negative hangover from those early days is that you cannot do anything medical with her. When clients used to come in saying they couldn't get their dog to take tablets or have flea treatment applied, I would think, 'Oh for goodness' sake, of course you can, let's just do this.' Oh no, I take all that back now. It is the one time Tilly will lose it and bite me, and as every dog owner will know, there is no reasoning with them once they have something they are stubborn about.

By then I had met the second of the three important Sri Lankan souls who were to really help make WECare what it is.

While I was treating as many animals by the roadside as possible, sometimes I needed to take them with me, and that wasn't always easy.

Most tuk-tuk drivers won't let you into their vehicle with the tiniest, healthiest dog, so try getting in one with a bloody or mangey dog – no chance. I'll flag them, they'll start to slow … then the second they see what you are about to ask, the accelerator goes down!

Then Chaminda came along. Malaka and I were stuck with a dog with an absolutely stinking maggot wound who needed to come back to the house for an operation, and Chaminda pulled up and didn't bat an eyelid.

'That poor dog, he needs help,' was all he commented, before we climbed into the back.

'You are the one.' I grinned to myself, and from that day onwards Chaminda – or Chaz as he is better known – became the third member of the WECare team. I paid him as I would pay any tuk-tuk driver for each journey, but he would prioritise our jobs over others, and at times was just solidly with us.

Believe me, he has had all sorts in his tuk-tuk since that day and never once complained. He just cleans the vehicle down, replaces covers when needed, and pushes on for the sake of his job and the dogs. An absolute legend.

So after that, it was the three of us out on the road together, and I would sit there listening to them chattering away in Sinhalese. Little by little it started to soak in, and I began picking up words, and then full sentences. It was important to me to learn the basics of the language for two reasons. One, I think it is respectful to locals, and it is so rare for a westerner to turn up knowing any of the language, that they appreciated the effort and it got us off to a good start. And two, if Malaka isn't around and I need to explain some basics to someone for the sake of the dog, I like to know I can. Oh and three, I can make sure they aren't taking the piss out of me!

In the beginning Chaz would just wait in his tuk-tuk, but over time he started picking up on what Malaka did, and would hand me things I needed too. The pair of them became so close that Malaka moved in with Chaz and his family.

It felt like everything was starting to fall into place and I was buzzing about it. Even though it couldn't have been further from life back home, I was no longer feeling out of my depth. In fact, if anything, the opposite was true – I felt really at home. Everything that was so abnormal was quickly becoming my normal, and the challenges were starting to feel possible to overcome.

CHAPTER SEVEN

IT'S A STREET DOG LIFE

I feel like I need to pause here to talk a bit more about street dogs, and actually get to the bottom of their existence, their day-to-day lives, and why after treatment I mainly return them to the streets – probably the question I have been asked the most over the years.

No one has ever been able to do a proper count for obvious reasons, but it is estimated that there are around three million unowned dogs in Sri Lanka – and that is before you include all the pets. When you consider that the population of people in one country is twenty-one million, that means there is a street dog for every seven people, so it is no wonder you feel like you see dogs everywhere.

They have been roaming the streets for decades, just kind of doing their own thing, and getting by in their own way. The government used to try and control numbers by culling the dogs. The law allowed that they could be rounded up and gassed or killed by injection, but thankfully in 2006 a 'No Kill' policy was brought in, and neutering and vaccination was seen as the much more humane, long-term, effective solution to what seemed to be an ever increasing population.

Street dogs come in all colours and sizes, although the most common look is small, brown, short-haired and wiry.

Pet dogs, on the other hand, are a real mix. They can be everything from little dogs from breeders, such as Pomeranians, who would have no chance surviving on the street, through to guard dogs. Unfortunately they are often caged, through fear of theft, or tied up outside the house twenty-three hours a day, with very little human interaction as their owners are a bit afraid of them. The owner/pet relationship I was used to back home isn't really the set-up out here.

It is important to understand that these street dogs are a very different kind of dog. Decades of fending for themselves means they are much closer to how dogs were before we domesticated them. They are independent, hardy, and need dog rather than human company.

For these street dogs, freedom is their number one need above all else, and to suddenly put them in a house and expect them to be happy with a daily walk would actually be very distressing to them.

It may not make sense to us, but they would choose the street over a warm fluffy bed in the house, because the street is their home. They will have their own community set-up, with an area that is their territory. They will have their daily routines, sources of food and water, and their friends and family.

So when we get asked why we put them back on to the street, strictly where they were picked up in the first place, the simple answer is that most of the time that is where they are happiest. They have come from generations of street dogs, and know nothing different, so why remove them from their freedom and their home?

But the one huge thing these dogs sacrifice by not being

owned is access to health care. Their lives are that bit grittier, riskier and dangerous, yet they have no real back-up plan, so the minute something goes wrong, they are in trouble. But because these dogs know no different, they just battle on. The injuries I have seen on these animals would break a pet dog elsewhere ... and on top of that a local will tell you, 'Oh yes, he has been like that for a couple of weeks.' It is incredible.

It can also be a bit of a vicious cycle, because the less health care a dog gets, the more sickness and disease they have, the less appealing they are to the locals. Fearful of catching something off these manky-looking dogs, they shoo them away, or stop them getting access to food or their homes. People worry that any contact might lead to them catching something nasty too, so the one time that a dog probably needs human intervention the most, he is the least likely to get it.

And that is where we come along ...

What always fascinates me is how well they accept the treatment. Despite the fact that these dogs will have had very little physical handling from humans in their lives, they are often much better behaved than my British patients. I definitely believe they are hardier and have a higher pain threshold, but they are also less likely to be divas about it!

Of course I have had plenty of bites over the years, but they are mainly just little warning nips, more to let me know 'Oi, that hurt!' rather than to intentionally cause damage.

Ironically the worst bite I have had off a street dog wasn't from an angry or frightened or aggressive dog, but an absolute sweety.

We had been looking after gorgeous Jimmy ever since we found him with two broken back legs. He had what is called a Robert Jones bandage on them – a common supportive splint to try and stabilise them while they healed.

We managed to get a lovely lady to adopt him, and I had been to her house to change these dressings loads of times, and he had always accepted it. He was a lovely boy and so sweet, and just lay there, no matter whether it was hurting him or not. But one day I was changing the dressings in his new garden when some monkeys went past in the trees above. Monkeys seem to wind the dogs up more than any other animal here, and they get excited and bark like crazy if one of them passes through their territory.

Well, Jimmy wanted to get to that monkey and, seemingly forgetting his broken legs and the fact the monkeys were up a tree, he decided I was the only thing between him and his target. So he whipped round, like 'Get off me!', and gave me a really bad bite of frustration on my arm. It wasn't meant maliciously, and he instantly looked shocked at his own behaviour and really guilty, like 'Oh gosh, what have I done?'

My arm bled loads and was really painful. We tried to patch it up as best we could as I had another dog I needed to get to. This was a Pomeranian with a perineal hernia who needed to be operated on. I was there with a head torch on as it was getting dark, in serious agony, stitching up this dog's back end, while trying to stop my own blood dripping down my arm onto my poor patient. I was so done in and desperate to get home. It was a pretty tough day.

I ended up with a nice scar from that, and in reality I should probably have gone to the hospital, but at the time I just figured I was up to date on all my jabs, and would let it heal by itself.

The one other time out here that I've hurt myself badly enough to need stitches, I stitched it up myself. I was surfing and had jumped on a rock and cut my leg, so when I got home I put steri-strips on it, and then a few little sutures. I used a local anaesthetic so I didn't flinch throughout and thought I was fine. I clearly wasn't as tough as I thought though, because then I passed out! One minute I was sat there talking, the next, embarrassingly, I came round lying there on the floor in my bikini. I'd still be inclined to do it again though, as knowing I have a good sterile kit to hand and the skills to stitch is very reassuring.

Anyhow, over time I have come to see what we call 'guardians' are the ideal solution for keeping an eye on street dogs.

A guardian is someone who doesn't own the dog, but looks out for it and steps in when needed. Some of the time we set up these relationships, but other times a person is already doing this. They take a back seat role, but it means there is someone who actually cares about the dog's welfare and can come to their help as necessary. They tend to know the dog's day-to-day routine (all dogs are total creatures of habit), so where they spend their time, the other dogs they get on with, and if they disappear off at times on adventures. They might also leave them out water and feed them.

As an aside here, dogs rarely live off dog food – even the owned ones – as it is so expensive to get hold of. They mostly end up with human leftovers which does the job just fine.

But the biggest thing a guardian can do is step in when there is a problem. So if they notice that a dog is suffering in some way, they do something about it. It might be a simple case of getting hold of flea treatment (available in the local supermarket) or, for more serious injuries, bringing them in to us. The idea is that as they know the dog, they can spot anything in its early stages and can flag it up to us for support before it becomes something bigger. Ultimately, they are like a friend to the dog.

If a dog already has a guardian and we are treating them we will try and locate the guardian, and if they don't have one, we will link them up with someone. As there is so little that needs to be done on a day-to-day basis, once you find a lovely person willing to do this role, there is no real limit to how many of the local dogs they can keep an eye on.

Top: My first true love, Finn. He was by my side for a blissful eleven years.

Bottom: Tom, the street dog I met on holiday who inspired me to start the clinic.

Top left: Joy, one of the dogs I met on holiday, was one of the first dogs I treated when I arrived in Sri Lanka.

Bottom: My little Ralphie, the first dog I adopted – he caused a drama when he was stolen!

Top right: Jeremy was picked up about twenty kilometres from the clinic. He was returned to where he was found but just kept coming back – now he often waits outside the clinic for some cuddles and fuss!

Top left: Chaminda became a vital part of the WECare team – he would prioritise our jobs in his tuk-tuk and never once complained about the smell!

Top right: Boris went on a little road trip to Colombo to be treated after I found him at the side of the road.

Bottom: Meeting Malaka for the first time. He was absolutely vital to helping to get the clinic started.

Top: Mali summed up what it was to be a street dog – he's probably my favourite street dog of all time.

Bottom: Dr Nuwar – another WECare superstar who was integral to the clinic's growth and survival.

Top: A CNVR (Capture, Neuter, Vaccinate, Release) clinic in full swing – they are hectic but crucial for the welfare of the street dogs.

Bottom: A tired but happy team after a busy day at an intense CNVR clinic.

Top: Benji was dumped on my doorstep, covered in mange – he totally stole my heart.

Bottom: Surfing is my escape from the worries and stress of running the charity – the waves wash all my troubles away.

Top: The clinic – the first space we could call our own and a reminder of how far WECare has come.

Bottom: Calamity George and Ticky chilling at the clinic – George quickly became the guardian of the clinic.

Top left: Ticky getting ready for some hydrotherapy in the sea – he hated it at first but it really helped him to get some movement back in his legs after he had been hit by a car.

Top right: With Amanda Holden after winning Vet of the Year at the Animal Hero Awards.

Bottom: My beloved Finn died shortly after I won the award – I vowed to help hundreds more animals in his memory.

Of course there are plenty of exceptions to this idea that living on the street with a guardian is the perfect set-up.

If a dog has been left with a lifelong disability or weakness that will make him too vulnerable for the street, we would try and find them a home. This might be an expat who I knew socially, or a friend of Malaka's. He would ask around the villages and find a kind-hearted soul who was willing to take in a new dog. We started to build up a bit of a network of the people who were dog lovers, and who would support us in what we were doing.

I also wouldn't put a dog back on the street if they had been with me for a particularly long time, as the chances are they will have lost their territory. From quite early on I settled on the cut-off point of three months, as then it is pretty much a guarantee that another dog will have taken over their area, and the last thing I want to do is start a turf war.

And then the other exception to the return-to-street rule is orphaned newborn puppies. WECare have ended up with puppies for a mix of reasons. Sometimes they are street dog litters whose mum has disappeared, other times they have been dumped by backstreet breeders. The law on dumping dogs actually changed while I was out there, making it illegal, and bringing in fines and even prison sentences, although it remains to be seen if this makes a difference.

I would never put a pup like this back on the street. Only about a quarter of puppies survive there to their first birthday and that includes those with mothers. A newly orphaned pup wouldn't stand a chance, so we need to find a new home for them.

If the puppy is a bit older though, I will return them in the same way as an adult dog, as long as they have only been with us a short time.

My favourite street dog of all time is called Mali. I think while most people coo over puppies, for me, the old dogs are the winners. They always seem so wise, and like they have really seen everything and are just sitting there with all their knowledge, watching everyone else make their mistakes!

The first time I set eyes on Mali was just before Christmas that first year, and I instantly knew he was one of those that had really seen life. He was sat in a village called Kalukatiya Watta, near where I had met Malaka the first time, outside a restaurant called Maliyada. His skin was in a dreadful state, mangey, cracked and broken, and he was absolutely covered in fleas. They were obviously distressing him so much that he was sitting on his bum on the concrete, turning in circles to try and scratch himself. We stopped the tuk-tuk and went over and he was instantly up, wagging and saying hello, a super-friendly dog even from that first visit.

I gave him flea treatment at the roadside, and spent a bit of time with him before we headed on. His name Mali came from two places – a shortened version of the restaurant he was outside, and also because, in Sinalese, Mali means 'mate' in a little brother kind of way. I'd heard Malaka and Chaz shouting it to each other in conversation, and thought it worked well for this wee dude.

After that we would spot Mali out and about most days, just busying about, doing his thing. We were told by the locals that he was eleven years old, which made him the oldest dog I had come across out there. To have survived on the streets all those years showed just what a smart chap he was.

I constantly tried to improve his skin, but he was a nightmare to treat, as he would always disappear when I wanted to do it. We needed to put the treatment on him weekly, but he would suddenly go AWOL when we were halfway through it, and reappear two weeks later, so we had to start it all over again. I didn't begrudge Mali heading off, though, as that independent spirit was exactly one of the things that made him so great.

So we tried to do baths with Mali instead. A lady on the road had taken a bit of a shine to him and semi-adopted him, and started acting as his guardian. She would let us bath him in her house, and although he made it clear he hated it, he was also a good boy and let us get on with it.

All of it was a bit of a lost cause in terms of improving Mali's appearance though, as he had been itchy for so long it was clear that his skin was pretty permanently damaged. He was never going to look anything but a bit mangey, even once he wasn't, as his hair just didn't have the ability to grow back properly. But the important thing was, the treatment was giving him some relief from the relentless scratching.

At another point we picked him up with a cut pad. I was worried about sedating him to stitch it up given his age, so we just put a local anaesthetic around it, and stitched it while he was awake. He couldn't have cared less. A quick lick of thanks, and he was on his way.

If there was any dog who summed up the street dog life for me, it was Mali.

CHAPTER EIGHT

CATCH, NEUTER, VACCINATE, RELEASE

While fixing up individual dogs was taking up a lot of time, I had still been plugging away at getting the vaccination and neutering programme off the ground, and we managed to get three sessions under way in those first six months.

They are called CNVR days – catch, neuter, vaccinate, release. It is a system that is used a lot around Asia and Africa, and does literally what it says on the tin. Dogs are caught from around the streets, neutered, vaccinated, and then released back to where they were picked up.

It has been happening in Sri Lanka since the tsunami when the Tsunami Animal People Alliance (TAPA), headed up by an American, started carrying out CNVRs. They are now working in partnership with Best Care Animal Hospital, and are still doing some work on the island, as is an organisation called Dog Star, which is run by a really pragmatic British couple.

After the government introduced the No Kill policy in 2006, they also began sending out CNVR teams. It is fantastic that it is happening, but they are just scratching the surface of what is needed, as there are so many dogs, so the more of this that can happen the better.

I was vaccinating all the dogs I was dealing with for other reasons, as I came across them, and neutering where possible.

Only Mali has really escaped the neutering, as I was worried about how well his body would handle it at his age and, to be honest, I'm not sure how much he has actually used his bits over the last few years anyway!

The first CNVR session that I managed to get off the ground happened just two months after I arrived in Sri Lanka and ran over two days. WECare put it on jointly with Embark, with us each funding one of the days. We settled on doing one day in Talalla, and the other in Kalukatiya Watta, where Malaka had been working his other six days in construction at the time. He was really keen that we do one there and it turned out to be a good suggestion.

You need a full vet team to carry out the work, and of course I had not created one of those for myself yet. Instead we hired a team from Colombo, who came along with their mobile unit and vehicles kitted out with equipment that allowed them to travel around to do these jobs.

It was quite an eye-opener for me as I watched them set up for the day, and head off to catch the dogs to bring them in for treatment.

The way it works is that a team of dog catchers will go off and collect any dog from the nearby area who doesn't have the corner of his or her right ear cut off – the universal sign that a street dog has been neutered. Called ear-notching, it might sound weird, but an obvious visual sign is needed to stop the same dog being picked up for treatment again. Some charities don't bother and rely on the scar on the dog to make it clear, but these can fade a lot over the years, especially if they were neutered as young dogs, and you don't want to have sedated them, or worse, even started the operation, before you find out they have been neutered before. It doesn't hurt the dog, as it is done while they are under anaesthetic, and the cut tip is cauterised.

The dog catchers use nets to catch the dogs for safety and speed. These are nets that are looped around a hooped opening, on the end of a long pole, almost like a long-handled fishing net.

The catcher needs to move quickly to get the net down over the dog, at which point he will often twist and wriggle, trying to escape, but the catcher will lift the net up so the dog is in the bottom, then twist the net to close the opening, and then pull it down to cover him. They might still struggle a bit, but by this stage it is more comfortable for them, and they can actually feel protected and reassured by the cover.

If a passerby doesn't realise what is being done, I understand it can look a bit brutal, but it doesn't hurt the dog at all, and actually most of them calm down and accept it, once they are inside the net. At the end of the day, a few distressing moments for a dog to be caught by a net is absolutely worth it for the treatment they are about to get.

The dogs are all loaded into the back of the van and brought to the central point, where the vets are set up ready to vaccinate them, and neuter them under anaesthetic. It can become a bit like a conveyor belt, but that is the best way to get through the most dogs possible in a day. Once they have come back around, they are released.

The release bit maybe sounds like a kind of afterthought, 'Oh yeah, and obviously let them go at the end,' but actually doing it right is a crucial part of the process. By that I mean keeping track of where each dog was picked up, and putting them back in that exact location. There are two main reasons for that. Firstly, as discussed before, the dog will have his own territory, possible guardian, other doggy mates, and even a family, so it is only right to drop him 'home'.

The second reason is for the health of the dog population as a whole. Moving sterilised and vaccinated dogs around opens up unwanted gaps where non-sterilised or vaccinated dogs can move in, effectively messing with the herd immunity situation that was being created, and potentially undoing the work.

During that first CNVR day in Talalla we set up in an open field area between the retreat and the beach. In a way I think running the day helped me with the local people, as it was quite a visual way of them seeing that I was putting WECare's money where my mouth was, and sorting treatment for the dogs on a bigger scale. It perhaps helped a bit in integrating me into the village.

I have a lot of love for the people in Kalukatiya Watta since that second day spent there, and have been back plenty of times since. While the ANI Villa hotel complex that Malaka was working on was really high end, the same can't be said for the lifestyles of the residents. It is quite a tough, gritty village, but the villagers are able to work together to create a simple but happy life, and once you have been accepted by the residents there is a lot of loyalty.

I helped out a bit during those first few days, but I didn't want to tread on any toes. It meant I felt a bit surplus to requirement during the sessions, as despite partially funding it I wasn't part of the actual team, so instead I just observed and made mental notes on the way I would improve it over time, when the chance arose.

I set up two more CNVR days using the same team from Colombo, but also began looking into costs and ways to run the entire operation myself. It was frustrating paying for vets when I was stood there as a vet not able to do anything, but knowing I could do these operations myself.

I thought the dog catchers could have done a bit more and scooped up a lot more dogs, but I also knew these guys were a close-knit team and it wasn't my place to suddenly start making demands and changes to how they worked. I realised if I was to really get to be hands on, I would need to create a team of my own.

As I researched further, I worked out that I could do a better job at a smaller price, as long as I could staff it, but that was my difficulty. While I knew other vets, I didn't know enough people with the relevant skills to form a CNVR team.

Well hellooooo there, helpful universe. After sending Malaka into my path, and then Chaminda, I was about to meet the third and final superstar who was to be absolutely key to WECare's survival and growth. Please welcome Dr Nuwan.

A vet I had met in Colombo told me about Dr Nuwan, a vet based in Gandara, just five minutes down the road from Talalla. They had studied together and he spoke highly of him. I mentioned him to a local British expat who said that he also knew Dr Nuwan and thought he did a good job, and he introduced us.

I think it is fair to say that veterinary as a choice of career is viewed very differently in Sri Lanka to the UK. Back home there is a battle over every place at vet school. It is super competitive and the absolute overriding factor as to why people go for it is a love of animals. In Sri Lanka, it is quite another matter. According to a professor I spoke with from the vet school in Peradeniya, near Kandy, 90 per cent of vets here originally wanted to be doctors and were trying to go down that route, but when they failed they got into vet school by default. As a result, for a lot of people the job is more about earning a wage, as opposed to a career where you are driven by an interest in animal welfare. I have even watched vets on several occasions who have not wanted to touch the animal they are treating, which makes the appointment practically futile. It is impossible to make an informed diagnosis without having your hands on the animal.

Obviously this doesn't apply to all vets, and there are some hugely dedicated and skilled vets across the country, and luckily for me Dr Nuwan turned out to be one of these.

From the first time we met I could see he was an extremely compassionate man with a real concern for the animals under his treatment. Money was a secondary issue to him – his first thought was about getting the job done properly and he was eager to help out WECare in any way he could.

A slim, quietly confident man of around forty years old, he was running his own successful clinic in the village and was focused on doing right by his clients there, so I appreciated the fact that he was also willing to show this interest in the street dogs.

The other thing that struck me was that while I sometimes found other professionals in my field could be dismissive of me as a westerner, and more particularly as a woman, Dr Nuwan always spoke to me on the same level. There was no issue if one of us told the other we disagreed with something, and we listened and were able to learn from each other's different areas of knowledge. As far as I am concerned, I am going to be learning things about animals and the vet profession until the day I die. Even the best vets on this earth don't know everything. So when people carry on like know-it-alls in a bit of an old boys' club, I find it really depressing. Dr Nuwan, though, was totally different and refreshing.

He very kindly said that when we had any operations to carry out, if we needed to do them on an operating table – as opposed to at the roadside or in my garden! – we were welcome to carry them out at his practice in Gandara.

But most crucially for what I was after at that time, he had been a government vet previously, and had carried out lots of CNVR campaigns in the north of the island. This meant he had access to trained people who I could put together into a team for my own, WECare-run, CNVR days.

It was ideal, and when I chatted with Dr Nuwan – or DN as we took to calling him – he was 100 per cent on board.

I couldn't wait to create our own teams that could be trained up in the way I wanted things to run, and introduce all the thoughts that had been running through my head when I had watched the previous CNVR sessions.

The biggest thing I wanted to change was the sterility of the process. People weren't always washing their hands, scrubbing into surgery, using kits sterilised in the autoclave (a pressurised container that steam cleans equipment), or changing kits between dogs. These were the absolute basic necessities of surgery for the safety of the animal and the success of the operations, but they weren't always being adhered to. I also introduced disposable drapes, as I didn't like fabric being used that had blood stains on it, having been washed in cold water. Even if it had been sterilised I still found it pretty gross.

My other big issue was the use of nylon for stitching up during operations. You may as well be using fishing wire, and is almost guaranteed to cause the animal future pain and discomfort. It has been contraindicated in the UK since the 1960s, but it is still available in Sri Lanka.

I showed DN how I wanted him and his team to use an absorbable suture material called catgut instead (weirdly actually made of collagen found in sheep and cow intestines, not that of a cat). This stays strong for a week, and then is slowly dissolved by the body's enzymes, and eventually disappears completely after ninety days.

As nylon is much cheaper – less than £10 a reel as opposed to £70–£80 for catgut – I could understand why it was still in use, but I wasn't comfortable with it. DN took this on board and incorporated it into his work, without question.

I didn't want to hugely change the format of the actual treatment the animal receives in the couple of hours they are with our team. One thing I was keen for though was a pre-op check, which I know slightly lengthens the process, but just ensures the dog is healthy for what they are about to go through. So, for example, I want a dog's heart checked before it goes under anaesthetic. What if it has a grade five heart murmur and no one bothered to investigate first?

The other bigger difference is I encouraged our team to try and give each dog more of a general 'MOT' at the same time.

Traditionally the focus has been so entirely on the neutering and vaccination that anything else gets ignored, or patched up to a very basic level. I understand why, as often the teams are on the road, their goal is one particular aspect of the animals' care, and they literally don't have the ability to take in injured dogs and deal with them beyond that day. But I could.

I was determined that if a dog came in with any other problems, we would tackle those too. Often this meant they might be on the treatment table for longer or that, if need be, they were coming home with me for more long-term treatment, but what was the point in sending them back to the streets neutered and vaccinated, but with an injury that would eventually kill them anyway?

As far as I am concerned these dogs may only see a vet once in their life, so you need to give them the best service possible, and send them back out to the road as good as new, prepared as best they can be to get through the next few years.

Yes, it's a bit more effort, and takes a teeny bit more time, but if it is better for the doggos, well that is what we are here for, so that is what needs to happen.

So with everything in place and running more as I wanted, we started doing CNVRs every couple of months with the new team of vets, assistants and dog catchers.

Those early ones were hard work. I was absolutely feeling my way, and trying to do what I saw best, and it didn't help that I struggled to get respect as a white, female boss. I would say something, and everyone would look to DN to see if that was correct. It was frustrating, but DN absolutely 100 per cent had my back, so that made it easier. But I had never been in an environment like it, and they just wouldn't look to me for answers.

Eventually I decided I just had to suck it up. I wouldn't go as far as saying I was accepting it, and it was to be an ongoing battle I would face out here, but I figured I had to pick my fights, and the ultimate goal was the dogs' welfare.

It helped that some of my vet friends from the UK had started to pop out when they could to volunteer for short periods, and it proved particularly useful in getting things running on these CNVRs. Word started spreading among those I had studied with, and then they told their friends, and people were keen to come out and help.

DN is the quickest surgeon I've met by a mile, and can fly through neutering procedures in no time, and with all hands on deck we aimed to treat seventy dogs in a day. Not bad going.

Malaka was once again invaluable, acting as translator and assistant, and working out what I would need and when, pre-empting any problem where possible.

He also had heaps of local knowledge and was really in tune with the countryside and nature, which proved to be useful in the oddest of ways.

Once when we were operating outside until really late, the moths were getting attracted to the lights hitting them, and falling into the open abdomen that I was trying to operate on. It was disastrous and I was getting really frustrated by it. Malaka disappeared for a bit, then came back with these leaves that he said would stop the moths and mosquitos. He hung them around the place and within minutes there wasn't a single one in sight. I love knowledge like that. We are useless at that in England, as everything has been made too convenient for us. You would just pop to the shop to buy a spray or something to deal with a problem, but actually we are over-complicating things and wasting money. It is interesting to see people make things work through good basic knowledge that we have lost, and improvise where we would just go and spend a fortune.

We made sure we did CNVRs in some of the places that felt a bit forgotten about in Sri Lanka, such as Nilwella. Stuck in between bigger, better-known areas, it gets a bit neglected. The population is mainly made up of fishermen, who spend long hours away from home, and where there is little time for education. So most of the kids don't bother with school but are roaming around on their own adventures, which I'm sure they are happy about, but also inevitably then leads to problems.

I really enjoyed our first CNVR there. We were set up by six a.m. and working in the heat, sweating all day. The locals were interested in what we were doing, and I will always encourage people to come and watch and ask questions. I loved that aspect of being out and about, in among the Sri Lankans, and I think they appreciated what we were doing for the dogs, as well as them, as healthier dogs makes for a healthier happier village.

A cute little kid came every day and would sit cuddling the puppies; he was really relaxed and natural with them. It turned out he had eight dogs at home and tried to look after all the street dogs in the area. He always had so many hanging around his home that his neighbours would get annoyed with him, but he was adamant that he needed to help them. I wanted to scoop this kid up myself and hug him. This is what the country needed, lots more children with hearts of gold and an affinity for dogs.

• CHAPTER NINE •

BELLE VERSUS A BOAR

The most valuable lesson I have learnt in the entire time I have been out here in Sri Lanka, came courtesy of a gorgeous dog called Belle.

We were alerted by one of the villagers in Gandara that a puppy had been attacked by wild boars. I hadn't really come across the boars by that stage, as they tend to keep away from the village, and people in general. They mainly live in long grass out in the fields and jungle and avoid interaction with humans, but an inquisitive dog can unintentionally run into them. On the whole the boar are quite shy, but it becomes a different matter if they have young and their protective instinct kicks in. Then, they are likely to go on the attack. I was surprised, as I had imagined them as being like harmless, hairy brown pigs, but it turns out that they can come up as high as your waist and have pretty vile temperaments. If I tell you they weigh as much as an adult man, and then add on the vicious tusks, you can imagine the serious damage they can inflict on a dog.

I headed over in the tuk-tuk, and found a six-month-old female street dog in a pretty bad way. She looked like she had been in a horrific car crash, and to be honest her whole body looked a real mess. The boar had really gone for her, sticking their tusks into the side of the puppy, and shaking her around, breaking almost everything on her left-hand side.

I asked who she belonged to, but was told she was a street dog, and that the family with her had just temporarily provided her with shelter to try and stop her suffering any more attacks.

Despite her obvious pain, she allowed me to handle her, so I was able to make an assessment on the spot and could see that her back leg was smashed to smithereens – her knee was dislocated, and there wasn't a single ligament left holding anything together. Her front leg had three fractures including one where the bone was sticking out, her tail was broken and she had wounds all over the place. In the UK there would have been no question of doing anything but putting her to sleep.

But this is Sri Lanka, and culturally things are different. The predominantly Buddhist religion of the country means euthanasia is a taboo subject, and the taking of a life, however good the intention, is believed by many of the locals to lead to bad karma.

This was an obstacle I had already found several times, as I needed the person responsible for a dog to agree to this course of action.

Until now, with the street dogs there were conversations, and compromises could often be reached. But ultimately, if a dog wasn't owned, their compromised welfare sometimes meant they had to be put to sleep. But suddenly the family who had been sheltering the pup decided she was definitely theirs, and would only hand her over on the basis I would operate and not euthanise. They said if I stuck to their terms, they would take her back home and look after her once she had recovered.

I felt I had no choice. I didn't have a clue what I could possibly do to give this beautiful dog a fresh chance at life, but I wasn't prepared to leave her there suffering. It was time to get creative.

Oh, how many times have I said that phrase during my time out here! 'It was time to get creative.' Perhaps that should be my mantra.

Carrying Belle, as I had named her, back home, I thought through the options. The problem was that I was looking at two bad legs. I wasn't hopeful that either could be saved, but I could hardly amputate them both and end up with a two-legged dog. Even the resilience of the Sri Lankan street dogs couldn't defy physics ...

I had built up a bit of a network of helpful specialists and vets from back in the UK who I bounced ideas off, and asked for advice. They were a mix of people from my university tutors, through to vets I had worked with, and they were all keen to share their knowledge with me whenever they could. This is a good thing about the UK veterinary industry – there are no egos involved when it comes to information sharing. We all want to pass on what we can and grow and develop as vets. It is for the good of the animals, after all.

So I emailed them all asking for their opinions, but not one of them was able to give me the magic solution I was hunting for. Instead all of them advised that the dog was a lost cause and putting her to sleep was the only way.

I really didn't want to do that, as I had made a promise and intended to keep it, so I carried on researching and thinking, while keeping Belle well dosed-up on pain relief.

Eventually I decided the best thing to do was amputate one leg, do my best to save the other, and hope Belle was a dog that could adapt to life on three legs, even if one of them was less than perfect.

Belle had already shown herself to be a bright and resilient little pup. Rather than lying there listlessly, she was watchful and interested, which gave me hope that she had the character to push through as best she could.

Her back leg was the worst, so taking a deep breath and hoping that I was about to prove everyone wrong, I amputated that one at the hip, then set about dealing with the injured front leg. An open fracture is at a massive risk of infection, so for the next six weeks I kept Belle in a bed next to mine overnight, so I could get up and give her intravenous (IV) antibiotics through the night, as well as strong pain relief.

Belle was an independent spirit, but slowly we bonded, and I couldn't believe it as each day she seemed to get a little better, and soon she was trying to stand.

She would hop around on her two fully functioning legs, using the third leg in its splint as support, then flop down, exhausted, in front of her food bowl to eat and drink.

As for her broken tail, completely fixing that isn't the easiest, as you basically need to keep it immobile. Find me a dog that doesn't like to wag their tail! So I made sure she was in no pain with it, and accepted that it would just have to set in whatever way it chose to. It wasn't like she needed a beautifully straight tail, and was an awesome-looking dog regardless.

As her injured leg became strong enough for the splint to come off, she grew in confidence. I'd initially kept Ralphie and Lottie away from Belle to allow her the space to recover, but after a while I didn't need to – it didn't matter that she only had the three legs, she could absolutely hold her own, and wasn't afraid to tell off any dog who came too close to her or became boisterous.

In fact, the more she was able to get around the place, the more demanding she became. She was adamant that I was predominantly hers, until I began to think of her as a bit of a diva!

Finally the day came when I decided Belle could go home to the family who had been keen to look after her.

It was bittersweet, as we had become firmly attached to each other, but I was glad to take her back to a family who had seemed to care. Yes, she now had three legs, and a bit of a wonky tail, but she was gorgeous, and loving and happy.

Except, it turned out, that wasn't good enough for them. Despite having warned them at the time that there was every chance if she survived it would be with three legs, when they actually saw poor Belle with her missing leg, they rejected her. I was heartbroken on her behalf, and angry that she was only deemed good enough when she was 'complete'. They had been so worried about her survival at the time that this lack of compassion was a bit of a shock.

I knew her missing leg would make it tricky to rehome her in general terms, and I was worried about putting her back on to the street after so long away. Her patch would have been long gone, so she would have had to fight to get one, and having been with us from such a young age, I wasn't sure how well she would fend for herself. There was nothing for it but to let her become another of WECare's permanent residents. That makes it sound very official, doesn't it? Basically, I mean another of the many dogs living with me! I now had Ralphie, Lottie, Benji, Tilly and Belle.

Belle seemed quite happy with this arrangement and became like an unofficial mascot of WECare Worldwide. She would bound around the garden with so much energy, and was well known to the local villagers, sometimes even coming with me on rescue missions, or heading off on one of her own adventures around the village on her three legs. They would call her 'Tuk-tuk' rather than Belle, likening her legs to the three-wheeled vehicle.

Despite my worries about how she would get on as a 'tripod', Belle was a street dog through and through. It was in her blood I guess you could say, and despite being given the option of living indoors, and having regular cuddles with me on the sofa, she would gravitate back out. She was not atuned to sleeping indoors, and you could tell that like many street dogs she found it almost claustrophobic. So I accepted that Belle loved spending time at the house and with me, but equally was often out and about doing her own thing, and seemed to be capable of holding her own.

I still kept a close eye on her and saw her most days, but every now and then she would disappear off for a few days at a time, and I would freak out, as I was sure something had happened to her. But then a villager would reassure me that they had seen 'Tuk-tuk' trotting around happily. And before you knew it, she was back to say hello, all cocky, as though she had been off on a holiday and having the best time ever. I imagined her on those trips as a lone wolf, an independent woman who doesn't take shit from anyone!

Not only did Belle's story work out well for her, but I can honestly say that dozens of other dogs' lives have been saved thanks to that little beauty. The lessons she taught me about giving a dog you think is past saving that last chance were immense. It had genuinely felt like euthanasia was the best and only option, until the family had me backed into a corner.

In the UK we see putting down badly injured dogs as the kindest thing to do, and there is no question that Belle would have been put to sleep that day if she had been brought to me at home. That idea, I guess, is partly influenced by cost. Belle's treatment would have cost around £5,000–£7,000 in the UK and, with only a small chance of success, it just isn't the decision anyone would make. That cost when I am working voluntarily for these dogs, though, isn't the same. What it cost WECare (if you ignore my time) was more like £300.

But regardless, I would have believed that there was practically zero chance of getting her a decent quality of life back. It was clear I was wrong, so it was time for a rethink.

It is all too easy for westerners to go to countries like Sri Lanka, so-called 'developing countries', and assume that our ways are right, or better. There are many times when it comes to veterinary care that I do still think that is true. But it is not a blanket rule, and actually there are times I've needed to sit back, listen, and assess and learn.

Just saying, 'years of study in our country have gone into this' isn't enough. I need to be open minded and see that sometimes there is another, better way. Giving things a chance has taught me so much.

Now I look at Belle charging around the place, and think how much spirit and life she has in her. Her resilience and positive outlook on life could probably teach most people a thing or two about the best way to live.

I am glad my hand was forced to operate on her, as now I assess the options for all dogs in a different light. While putting to sleep is sometimes the kindest choice, a good quality of life is possible in many more circumstances than we often realise. I know plenty of dogs that have come after Belle are only here because she taught me not to underestimate them and that they might surprise me. If at all possible, it is only fair to give them a chance, even if it might feel like an impossible challenge.

In the end, I think it is fair to say that Belle helped me as much as I helped her. Having her come into my life was an absolute game changer for my Sri Lankan life, and the potential impact of WECare.

CHAPTER TEN

JET-SETTING VET

L iving might be pretty cheap, but it didn't mean I wasn't getting through the £10,000 pretty quickly: dog food, medicine, equipment and wages all added up. Since my arrival I had been sure to try and top the money up where possible, so it didn't completely disappear.

I had initially been working one day a week with an animal hospital called Best Care, who treated owned dogs near the capital. I'd go to their inpatient facility, where they could have up to fifty dogs at a time receiving ongoing treatment, and spend time with each of the dogs. Then I'd come home and draw up a plan of action for each of them to pass on to the vets. It was a lot of work for little pay, and there was less equipment at their disposal than I would have liked, but the vet at the inpatient facility was a brilliant guy. He was so receptive and trying his absolute best with the dogs.

Then I began doing talks and presentations to several of the clinics, on different areas that I hoped would be useful to vets.

So things such as ultrasonography, or how to do neurological examinations, as they were seeing a lot of spinal injuries. I also spoke on how you scan a spleen and a bladder, or the best way to carry out hernia repairs.

I did a talk to fifty-two government vets who work in neutering clinics, on basic surgery skills. They were asking questions such as, 'Can you show us how to do cataract surgery?', while I was adamant about bringing the conversation back around to the importance of hand washing before surgery! I am sure they were irritated that I was so focused on the basics, but seeing people skip that simple routine drives me crazy, and it can cause so much damage if ignored. Generally I really enjoyed the talks and getting to share knowledge with others. It also allowed me to gain a better understanding of how veterinary care worked in Sri Lanka.

But one of the absolute best bits about going to do these talks near Colombo was the chance to get on one of the island's buses. They are unlike any bus I've come across before. The second I set foot on the bottom step to climb on, the bus was off, and I was clinging on for dear life as I worked my way gingerly down the aisle. There was no sitting in the front row – those seats are reserved for the clergy. Once I'd found a spot, I looked along the brightly decorated bus, adorned with all sorts of religious iconography, with the high point of a buddha surrounded by flashing lights at the front.

A kid with a money bag made his way over to sell me my ticket but it was a case of communicating by sign language as the traditional-style music blaring out of the speakers, accompanied by a music video on screen, made it impossible to actually hear each other.

It was such a funny, party, young-people kind of vibe, yet the bus was filled with the middle-aged and elderly, off out for a day's shopping!

If you are lucky enough to be on board when the bus passes through one of the main stations, there's the chance to buy nuts or fruit from one of the sellers who jump briefly on board. There is also supposedly the time to go for a toilet stop, but there's no chance I'd take that risk – the driver wouldn't think twice of heading on without you.

It sounds insane – it IS insane – but you can't help getting off one of those buses in a better mood than you got on. And when a journey is less than £1, it was a great way to travel when I was trying to save every penny.

I also tried to keep the cost of equipment and medication as low as possible by sourcing it as donations or at a reduced cost, as well as applying for grants. So, for example, we were given one to pay for nets to catch dogs during the CNVRs. We occasionally use them at other times as well because despite our best attempts not all dogs are willing to be handled. You get the very occasional one who just cannot be caught and will want to bite, mainly out of fear.

From day one, I put WECare's story out on social media, partly to let people know what we were doing and raise awareness, and partly in case anyone wanted to donate. I posted about the work on a lot of Facebook groups for people in the veterinary profession, and asked if they could consider us when they had any spare out-of-date medicine. Everything in the UK that is used in the veterinary profession has a best-before date. But unsurprisingly this date generally veers hugely on the cautious side. So while out-of-date stuff can't be donated within the UK, even to charity, I discovered that it can be passed on abroad – and I was more than happy to snap that up. The same goes for dog food.

I always use my discretion with these meds though, and use them for the less critical cases. So say I came across a dog with heart failure, I was only going to use in-date meds. But for a dog with a little wound, I might try the out-of-date antibiotics first, and know that in two days if they don't seem to be working, it's not the end of the world to then change them.

It obviously isn't the ideal situation, but equally it is about doing what I could to stretch the money out for as long as possible, to extend the work of WECare, and ultimately to save as many dogs as possible.

Anyone who came over to volunteer would fill their suitcases with some of this stuff to save us the postage, and then knew to look out for any opportunities for me once they were back in the UK.

It still wasn't enough though, and the money was disappearing too quickly, so in the end I decided I needed to head back to the UK for a work stint to earn some money, spend as little as possible while there, then get back out to Sri Lanka.

It was strange being back in the UK. Everyone and everything was the same, but felt different to me. It was lovely to see my family and friends again, and of course my beloved Finn, but I also felt a bit removed from it all. My home had been with Alex, but now that didn't exist any more, I felt a bit like a tourist to the area. It was also really bloody cold and grey!

It was nice to be back in Westway earning money, and I loved dealing with clients again in the surgery, but the downside was that everyone now seemed super neurotic to me. Someone would rush in with 'an emergency' and it would turn out to be a simple eye infection. I would stand there in amazement, thinking of what the dogs were going through in Sri Lanka, and wonder what on earth was going on with these overly pampered pooches! After everything I had witnessed in Sri Lanka, I just kept thinking these guys should appreciate what they had.

It became clear just how much the recent months had changed my attitude as a vet too. So while I tried to fit back into the UK vet culture, there were certain things that stuck with me, in particular what I had learnt from Belle – more dogs than you think can be saved, rather than needing to be put to sleep.

One morning I was asked to see a couple whose dog had been referred for euthanasia by another vet, and I was due to carry this out. I assessed the dog, and looked at the large mass that had developed on her neck.

'I'm really sorry, I don't want to rock the boat when you have made the decision, but I think we could have a crack at fixing this.'

The couple were shocked, but their dog went into surgery and, sure enough, she recovered and lived for three more years. The owners kept in touch and told me, 'Thank goodness we saw you, or she would have missed out on all that extra life.'

It was only thanks to Belle that I had learnt to give animals more of a chance. Her impact was spreading across the globe.

I'm not sure what my colleagues thought of the new me. I know they were constantly having to remind me to actually use the equipment to help with my job. I'd be there diagnosing a broken limb by touch, and they'd be like, 'Erm, Janey, you know there is an X-ray machine down the corridor that can tell you for sure, right?'

I'd got used to relying on my senses a lot more, and my examination skills had shot up as a result. I hadn't been able to rely on diagnostic tools to tell me what was up in Sri Lanka, but had worked out all my own tricks and techniques instead. Of course the machines can tell so much more, and having some of them out there with me was on my future wishlist (keep dreaming, Janey), but in the meantime I was pleased I had become so self-sufficient.

I am glad I did that stint, but I was surprised just how keen I was to get back to my Sri Lankan doggies. I also found it tiring trying to juggle the work I needed to do in the UK for WECare –

seeing donors, corporates who might donate equipment, applying for grants, etc. – along with the vet work. So after that I decided UK visits would only be focused on work for the charity, and spending time with people (and a dog) that I cared about.

The next time I needed to up the funds, I emailed a few clinics in Dubai, Hong Kong and Singapore. They are closer than the UK, so flights are cheaper, and also I knew I would just put my head down and work – the distraction of family and friends wouldn't pull me away.

A clinic in Dubai were the first to get back to me, and I went over as a locum for two weeks. Can you imagine three more different places to work, in terms of dogs and the treatment of them, than Sri Lanka, the UK and Dubai?

The clinic is run by an Aussie and a Brit, and most of the staff are western, so that is reflected in their standards and approach. But that is where the similarities to back home end. The caseload and the clients couldn't be more different.

Generally Emiratis are some of the nicest people I have met, extremely caring about their animals, as are the many expats who live out there. They will come in at all hours if they are worried about their animals, and money is rarely an issue.

But you have to be very careful as you have no idea who your client is. In that respect I felt sorry for my bosses, as it is a lot of pressure. Keep a sheikh waiting for two minutes, or speak in a manner they don't like, and they can have the clinic shut down instantly. Inversely, get it right and you are treated very well. We treated one of the sheikh's dogs out of hours once, and he came and gave each of the nurses 6,000 dirhams – around £1,300. A nice bonus.

Having said that, the more upper class the people, the less likely they are to come in themselves, but will send a maid or driver with their pet. This can be frustrating, as that person doesn't always speak the best English, and once you have taken the time to go through everything and make yourself understood, they just say, 'Let me call Madame,' as ultimately they don't have the power to make any decisions. That just means we have to do the consultation all over again by phone. When the whole appointment is supposed to happen in fifteen minutes, it is not easy, and does add time pressure.

Other times the client won't send money with the maid or driver. So although they will say, of course they are happy to pay the 2,000 dirhams and to go ahead with the operation as money is no issue, you then have to spend all day chasing that payment. It is another world really.

One frustrating aspect is the idea that everything is in God's hands as opposed to humans needing to make decisions. So the response to a lot of questions is, '*Inshallah*', i.e. 'God willing'.

I completely understand this sentiment as a way to understand that bad things happen, and we need to accept that much of life is out of our hands, as well as death. But at other times it is down to us to make a decision that can determine the outcome.

The most common animal we see there is cats. They are brought in with injuries from falling from one of the high-rise buildings, or jumping off balconies, or they have been caught in tower fires, injured in a road traffic accident (RTA) or have renal failure. There are lots of street cats, so issues that are easily spread through cat to cat contact are common, such as FIV (similar to HIV) and FeLV (feline leukaemia virus). Then you get plenty of dogs and house pets, but also more unusual animals such as sugar gliders – super-cute little creatures, kind of like flying squirrels. We aren't called in as vets to see the camels or horses though – the Sheikhs have their own vets specifically working on those animals.

I had heard all the horror stories before going, and I am sure if you dig deeper there are some very real concerns over treatment of the lower-paid workers, such as labourers and maids. But the crazier stories that get covered in the media, such as a man going to jail for touching another man's hip, don't reflect the reality that I saw. I am aware I was there in the ex-pat bubble, which is shiny and protected, but I did feel safe and enjoyed my time working there. It also made for an interesting, almost direct contrast to Sri Lanka, and made me appreciate aspects of both countries.

So since that first trip I have gone for a couple of weeks every six months, to work my backside off for twelve days straight, ideally with as many night shifts as possible for the double pay. I'll stay with a friend and, as the wage is similar to the UK, but tax free and with a cheaper flight, it definitely makes it worthwhile.

One amusing thing about my time in Dubai (although not so funny at the time) is what I have managed to catch there. In the entire time I have been in Sri Lanka, despite everyone's fears about all the so-called infectious diseases that the dogs are riddled with, I have only caught a mild case of one thing and, to be honest, that was entirely my own fault. Unfortunately, I can't say the same for Dubai! Remember I said that mange on the whole can't be passed on to humans? Well, effectively there are two types of it: Demodectic mange (or Demodex) is the most common, but then there is Sarcoptic mange, which is the one that humans can catch. Demodex is caused by a normal cigar-shaped mite that lives on a dog's skin, but when the dog is ill or immunosuppressed, it begins to cause them problems. That is why you will see it on pups who haven't had the best start in life, as when they are suckling, the skin-to-skin contact sees it passed on from mum, but their bodies aren't ready to handle it.

Sarcoptic mites are little round mites that are passed on by contact, and burrow into the skin. These mites do not survive long term on humans, but it can cause irritation for a short while.

The only way to medically tell which type a dog has is to take a skin scrape and look at it through a microscope, but even then it isn't easy. A dog may have both types, and whereas the Demodex type is easy to spot, the Sarcoptes mites are little buggers, and will hide themselves away out of sight.

You can take a blood test too, to determine the mite, but to be honest as the treatment is pretty similar it seems a waste of money and time to do that, nice though it is to know what you are dealing with.

When I took in Benji, after he was dumped out the front of my house as a puppy, I couldn't resist letting him sleep in bed with me. He was so small and lost that I wanted to keep him warm and comforted. Not a medically smart decision when he had mange, I know, but I couldn't help myself.

It was maybe no surprise that he had Sarcoptes mange and I then caught it. It presents as a form of scabies on humans, but as the mites cannot live very long on human skin, it is self-limiting and luckily didn't spread too far in the two weeks I had it.

But then ... two pet rabbits were brought to me in Dubai with mange. I took them upstairs to the treatment rooms, put gloves on, and got them out of their cage. I'd barely touched them during the treatment, but wow, the itchiness I was suffering within hours!

I was absolutely covered in scabies, from my bum all the way up across my chest. It was all over my stomach in this horrible hive-style rash that I just Could. Not. Stop. Itching.

It is normal to see a dog scratching, whichever type of mange they have, but the Sarcoptes one is reputed to be worse, and at that moment I felt the pain of those dogs. The need to itch was off the scale.

As a heads-up, most cases of mange in the UK are the Sarcoptes type – the kind that will get you itching too – so if you suspect this on your dog, take real precautions, and see a vet as soon as possible.

I think I caught scabies in Dubai as for some reason the mange there is super strength! But also I was so run down and my immune system was perhaps unable to fight much, because just a couple of weeks later I caught ringworm. Despite growing up on farms I'd never had that either, so I think my body was trying to tell me to look after myself.

I'd been helping a street kitten in Dubai – there aren't really street dogs in Dubai, but there are plenty of stray cats – and, like an idiot, took it into my house to sort it out. Before I knew it, I had these angry red circles on my face and my chest. They weren't as bad as other people's – they weren't itching, and my poor friend had one that ulcerated under her arm – but mine just looked awful. I had been on a couple of dates with this guy and he asked if it was ringworm. 'No!' I blurted out, embarrassed, but the poor guy was grossed out, realised I wasn't exactly being truthful, and that was that!

Once I had something where my armpits went black. Do not ask me what it was, it was super weird, and really sore – I even carried out CPR on a cat with wet paper towels tucked under my arms, as all I could think about was the pain.

Given that I think of Dubai as being a sterile, super-hygienic place, it was bizarre I caught everything there, rather than in Sri Lanka where you would assume the chances are higher. Just goes to show that everyone was worrying about these street dogs for no reason.

CHAPTER ELEVEN

CULTURE CLASHES

I get it, dogs aren't everyone's number one priority in life. You are even allowed to not be particularly fond of dogs (although to be clear, if you don't, you are obviously untrustworthy and selfish, and we will never be friends …!).

In all seriousness though, I understand that people often have other things to think about. Sometimes they are just struggling to get by themselves, or to raise a family on a pittance. While extreme poverty isn't actually that common in Sri Lanka, the living standard is still pretty low, and there are plenty of people living without access to things such as electricity, who are trying their hardest every day to make ends meet and get by. Someone once said to me, 'Offer a Sri Lankan one pound today, or ten pounds if they wait until Friday, and they will take the one pound every time.' That is not a criticism, but a reflection of the instability of life here. Of course it simplifies it, but life is much less certain and who knows what will have happened by Friday so people end up taking life one day at a time.

Much of that way of being has come about because, put simply, Sri Lankans have had a pretty tough time of it in recent years. First there was the twenty-six-year-long civil war between the government and the Tamil Tigers. People feared being caught up in attacks, were unable to travel freely, and a shocking 100,000 people were killed over the years. It was a shadow hanging over the country until they finally came out the other side with peace declared in 2009.

Then there was the horrific 2004 Asian tsunami that killed 35,000 Sri Lankans, and swept away countless homes and businesses, destroyed farmland and tourism. I've watched videos of the water sweeping in across the south of the island that I know and love, and it brings tears to my eyes imagining the fear and confusion everyone must have felt at the time. Flooding and mudslides have also caused regular disasters since.

As you would expect, both the man-made war and the natural disasters have left their scars on the country – physically, psychologically, emotionally, and financially.

So I absolutely understand that buying flea treatment for a dog isn't always a priority. I'd never judge someone on that front. As long as they aren't actually being cruel, I can completely accept that in reality a lot of people have something else to focus on.

For the same reason I have changed my thinking about other aspects of dog care, such as the food. After years of being used to serious, considered debates on what to feed a dog, I really think the answer is: whatever you can. Dried food, rice and fish, raw food, curry … whatever. I'm obviously not suggesting a diet of chips and cake is ideal, but the important thing is that the dogs get fed in the first place. The irony is, while I have always ordered in dog food for my dogs, for some reason the street dogs have way better teeth than any of mine, so I've given up questioning the food they might get. And let's face it, hardly any humans in the East or the West eat the optimum diet, so let's not worry if dogs don't get the perfect diet either, when there are so many out there who need care on a much more basic level.

But there is one cultural difference around dogs I have come across in Sri Lanka that I have spent a lot of time considering, but have real difficulties accepting, and that is a refusal to euthanise. For me, a dog's welfare comes first and foremost, and sometimes that absolutely has to involve putting an animal to sleep.

When you train to be a vet in the UK, there is what is known as the Five Freedoms that every animal should have the right to. They are:

> Freedom from thirst, hunger, and malnutrition
> Freedom from discomfort and exposure
> Freedom from pain, injury and disease
> Freedom from fear and distress
> Freedom to express normal behaviour

They all sound pretty basic and straightforward, right? Choosing to deprive an animal of any of those is when basic welfare issues come in and you can expect potential prosecution. Equally, if the animal ends up in a situation where the above can't be achieved because of injury or bad health, that is when euthanasia is considered.

As well as the obvious reasons such as pain and discomfort, dogs can end up at the vets with conditions that mean they will never be able to feed themselves or walk again. If a dog has lost half their jaw thanks to explosives (like Rosie, p.7), and it cannot be rebuilt enough that they will ever be able to eat again, do you leave them to a life of tube feeding, or maybe let them just waste away? If attempts to fix two shattered legs have failed, and the dog will never be able to move around again, do you leave them stuck in one place for the rest of their life? If maggots have eaten through a dog's eye into the brain before they reach you, should the outcome be left to nature?

These are all circumstances I have faced in Sri Lanka, where it is clear to me that the dog is not getting the Five Freedoms, nor is there any way that I can make them a reality for the poor pup again. In these situations, it is clear that it is cruel to let the animal carry on living and I believe euthanasia is the only kind step.

Unfortunately, my beliefs and the local beliefs do not always match up in this area, mainly because of a way of thinking that comes from the Buddhist religion, the dominant religion of the country.

The belief is that you should never kill, and that if you do so it creates a negative karma that will result in a worse suffering, either in this life or the next. The thinking is that nature needs to be left to take its course, and while you should offer the animal comfort, and help to relieve suffering, you should not take any action to shorten their life. Within the religion there seems to be a spectrum of how strictly this is adhered to, but the more orthodox followers pursue the idea that no matter what, you never, ever interfere by removing life.

This is really problematic for me. While much of what I have seen here has adjusted my way of working to look less to euthanasia – Belle being a prime example – I am a huge believer that there are times when it really is the only option.

Equally, I strongly believe in not going to a country and trying to impose western beliefs and ways of life. I'd rather it was a two-way relationship. That everyone approaches things with an open mind, and perhaps we can learn from each other's culture. I have tried to be respectful in every way possible, and take on board local cultures and ideas across the board. Everything from not wearing shoes indoors, to being aware of how unnecessary so many material possessions are, have filtered into my everyday life.

But where I have struggled to compromise is when it comes to animal welfare. I just cannot leave a dog to struggle on through pain. It goes against all my instincts as a vet, a dog lover, and an empathetic human.

Some of the charities on the island have taken this idea that euthanasia is forbidden as gospel, and don't put down a dog no matter how much pain it is in, or how non-existent its quality of life may be. But I wasn't willing to give up, and instead have managed to find ways to communicate and compromise, in nearly all cases.

The first time I realised just how possible this was, I was called out to a dog who was under a tractor and had apparently been hiding there for months, chewing off his own feet. They were filled with maggots, and he was beyond saving. But the nearby people didn't want me to put him to sleep. They kept arguing that perhaps he was paying for a sin in a previous life and to interfere would be to increase the animal's suffering in the next life. That's completely inhuman in my mind and goes against every kind thing that Buddhism represents. Why would you want a dog to suffer?

Malaka and I spent two hours discussing it with one particular man, going into detail about everything, and putting in the time and effort to explain our side of things. Eventually he came round, and it felt like my first big win on that front, and made me realise that what might seem like a lost cause, with a reasoned conversation can often end with the best outcome for the animal.

It is only about twice a year that I am met with a point blank 'no', where I have not been able to come to an agreement, and those situations break my heart. Leaving an animal with someone when you know it is not the best thing for them is the worst feeling in the world. But it is not like the UK, where I'd have the backing of the RSPCA and could overrule beliefs with science. Here a person's beliefs take priority and I would be prosecuted for theft if I took the dog.

It's shit, and the absolute hardest thing to walk away. The only way I can try to justify it is if I don't respect that is the way of the country, I'd not be able to stay and look after all the other dogs. At that moment, though, it doesn't feel right at all.

The rest of the time, luckily, while we may be starting the conversation from opposite ends of the spectrum, quiet discussion of the pros and cons has led to a lot of people coming to the conclusion that euthanasia is okay in a particular situation. No one wants to see a dog suffering, so if you can offer them a reasoned explanation, more often than not people are open to it.

One successful option I have found to put people's minds at ease is to get the dog signed over to me. If an owner gives me the dog and we agree it is now mine, that effectively takes away the karmic responsibility, and allows me to make what I believe is the right choice.

Fortunately, I think the beliefs across the country are moving towards being more open to euthanasia, and will hopefully continue in that direction. I spoke to a monk in one of the local temples on the topic recently, as I was keen to get an understanding of it from the perspective of a religious figurehead. I was lucky to be chatting to a forward-thinking monk, who was just twenty-one years old.

I asked him about the idea that it caused bad karma to put an animal to sleep, and his response was, 'Karma comes from intentions, not actions, so if you intend to relieve the suffering of an animal, then that is a good thing, we should do it.'

He explained that he believed that as long as a person's intentions were genuine, and that it was solely about the animal's welfare and reducing suffering, as opposed to a person's own sentiments or ease of life to no longer have to care for the dog, then it made sense to opt for euthanasia.

I was really impressed with him, and felt that if he was representative of the direction Buddhism was taking in the country, it aligned really well with my own values and those of the clinic and, more importantly, would be beneficial to the dogs.

I also asked him about neutering, as we get some people saying that is a sin. There is no real basis for the argument, but it tends to be more something people say when they aren't sure what side to take. As a friend pointed out, Buddha wasn't here when neutering was an option, so why would he have expressed an opinion on it? It is all about interpretation. Interestingly, this same monk said he believed in neutering, and what we were doing with the dogs was exactly right. Phew!

On a side note, I used the same conversation to bring up two elephants that are chained up at the temple in the nearby town of Dondra, a fact that constantly horrifies me, and thousands of tourists who have come across them. They are there for use in traditional ceremonies, such as the monthly full moon celebration called Poya, and then the hugely impressive Perahera – or The Festival of the Tooth. Apparently this has its roots in the fourth century, and is meant to encourage rainfall and rich crops across the country. It is a huge ten-day festival filled with colour, musicians, jugglers, fire breathers, dancers and, of course, elephants, dressed up to the nines, who parade through the streets. An incredible sight? Absolutely. Kind to the animals? Definitely not.

When the elephants are not taking part in parades, they are kept at the temple to draw in tourists, who are encouraged to pay for photos with the animals. But while people constantly visit thinking they will see happy elephants, they quickly leave upset, as the elephants are on short chains in the sun, swaying with distress, unable to lie down, and exhibiting all kinds of signs of trauma. It's a very cruel set-up.

It breaks my heart that a religion that we associate so closely with being caring and kind to all doesn't always seem to extend this empathy to all living creatures.

Again, though, chatting to this lovely monk, it seemed that there is potential for much of this abuse to change. He said that a lot of the younger monks had complained to the older ones about the situation, and had asked that when these two elephants die, that they are not replaced.

In the meantime, though, as these two have been here since they were born, they can't just be released into the wild, as they wouldn't know what to do.

While I'd still like to see them living out their days in a nice paddock, I appreciated the thought process was at least happening, and change does seem to be on the horizon.

• CHAPTER TWELVE •

AN ACTUAL CLINIC

It probably comes as no surprise to anyone that my one year anniversary in Sri Lanka came and went without me even really noticing. I guess I must have known from pretty early on that this wasn't just going to be a sabbatical from my UK vet job. This was a new life that was going to be mine for the foreseeable future. Setting up this charity and then walking away from it and leaving all the dogs without help just wasn't an option. I was nowhere near finished, and who knows if I ever will be.

Luckily the idea of returning within a year hadn't been set in stone with my bosses at Westway, and as they had been involved in the charity along the way, they could see that this wasn't just a whim, or an itch I was scratching, it was bigger than that, so they didn't hold me to it.

In some ways, it seemed like I have been out here for ever. Everything from the smell of cooking dosa and roti, to the tinny sound of Mozart music that announced the bread van on his daily rounds, were part of my daily life and had soon become my 'normal'.

But equally, the time had flown by and it was frustrating, as I didn't feel I'd made as much progress as I wanted with the dogs. There had been so many pitfalls and issues I had never envisaged, and I'd had to spend so much more time on paperwork, problem solving, and trying to raise further funds, than I had ever imagined.

I missed Finn and my family, and even though I talked to my mum on the phone, it obviously wasn't the same. I never wanted to tell her everything, as when you are having a catch-up you don't want to be unloading all your problems.

As for friends, I had such a great bunch of them back home, but just hadn't been able to build up the same connections in Sri Lanka.

I have met some absolutely brilliant people, but the expats tend to come and go. People will be out here for six months, but then head off on the next adventure, or feel the pull of home, and just as you are getting to know someone properly, they are off. Any who are here for longer are focused on the business that has drawn them out here in the first place, and friendships are secondary. I count myself in this, and worry that I didn't – and still don't – have the time to be a good friend to anyone, as the dogs are everything.

Then there are the locals. I have developed some fantastic relationships with many Sri Lankans, but the language barrier, in spite of a basic ability of getting by, obviously gets in the way of forming deeper friendships a lot of the time.

Also the area of the country I am in is very traditional in its thinking. Very few women work, but are instead at home looking after children, the house, and cooking (making the most incredible meals, made entirely from scratch each day, I have to add!). But this allows little chance to meet or develop friendships, and they are all very bemused at my friendships with males, as it is not really the done thing.

Knowing that some of my best girlfriends over the years have come through sports teams, I tried joining a netball team. The Sri Lankan women won the Asian Championships, and are really good netballers. But try training in the one p.m. sunshine … I honestly thought I was going to have a heart attack and immediately felt like a very embarrassed, unacclimatised westerner!

I also tried messaging everyone I knew to get a weekly beach volleyball session going, but that never took off. The only recreation that seems to be constantly available on tap is yoga, and that's all well and good, but it is the craic of a team sport that I need.

It is lonely. There is no doubt about it.

The one sport I do try and find time for is surfing. It is a real solo sport, so doesn't help on the social front, but it has been great in helping my mental health. It might sound cheesy, but out on the waves the troubles can feel like they are being washed away, and I'm in my happy blue sanctuary. However bad life feels when I go out on my board, it feels a million times better when I finally head back in for land.

By now, my house was overflowing with dogs. You couldn't sit on the sofa, without first having to shift a few to make space, and I worried the neighbours might object to some of the late night barking. There were no less than thirteen dogs in my house at any one time. Even for a crazy dog lady like me, it was getting too much. It also meant that I was never away from work, as I would be treating any number of them through the night. It was reaching breaking point.

Malaka would help out, taking some of the dogs to his place, but he could see my house was still bursting at the seams, so he found us a kind of garage area to rent, with land at the back. It was only £50 a month, and a few of the dogs started living there, and I was able to put some of the more poorly ones there overnight in crates. We did some bits of surgery on the floor in there, but it was a horrible place, and didn't feel like we had taken a step forward, more that we were making the best of a bad situation.

The upside was, I was starting to feel like I was getting a bit of my house back, and I took the time to make it a bit more homely, so that I could come back and relax in a place that felt more like my sanctuary at the end of the day.

I was keen for Malaka to keep up the search for a new place to replace the garage, with the idea that we could eventually upgrade to what could even one day be a proper clinic. The boy – of course! – came good, and soon enough turned up with exciting news: he had found us an actual real base. A place where WECare could put down roots, and where I could treat the animals without having to do things in the middle of the street, the depressing garage, or in a makeshift set-up in my home.

Malaka had come across a building just outside Gandara that had previously been used as a small school. It had a large garden for the dogs with high walls on all sides which might not sound like a big deal, but actually very few properties in the area had proper boundaries. Even people's gardens generally flow into each other, or are just divided by a couple of bushes, barbed wire, or some rickety corrugated iron.

It was nowhere near being my perfect clinic venue – I had a whole long list of dream requirements for that – but it was a million times better than the current set-up. I could see that there was some real potential for the place, at least as a stopgap, and I started to get excited, imagining what I could do with it. We agreed rent at £200 a month, and that was it – in January 2016, WECare had its first actual clinical base.

I remember the first time I walked in, once it was ours. It was so amazing to have a space to call our own, and felt like we were finally moving towards becoming a legitimate, established charity. But I was equally aware of just how far we still had to go.

Effectively we had the shell of a clinical base, which meant while there was a lot of work to be done, we had a blank canvas to design it as we wanted.

I roped in a bunch of mates in the area and we got stuck in painting walls, clearing the garden, and making the whole area safe and dog friendly. The main focus internally was making sure it was clean and sanitary.

I kept Ralphie, Lottie, Benji and Tilly at home, as they were my pets, and transferred all the other patients. Belle moved to the clinic too, as she liked the extra space, and was a bit too territorial of me as far as the others back home were concerned. She was still really affectionate with me, but didn't like other dogs giving me too much attention, and would come charging over as though to say, 'Get off her, she is my mum, I was here first!'

We didn't have the funds to kit out the clinic for now, but it was a relief to have the space. It did mean that we were making do with the most incredibly basic set-up. For a good while we were literally having to carry out surgery on the floor. Often we had no lights, and there were no sinks, and definitely no air conditioning. I still didn't have many of the items that would be deemed necessary basics by most vets. I dreamt of the day I could get my hands on X-ray and ultrasound machines. I was still doing everything by feel, from working out breakages to assessing pregnancies. Techniques that might work a lot of the time, but were less than ideal.

But we had boxes of towels, food, basic meds, and heaps of enthusiasm, dedication and love for these dogs. And let's face it, it was still a step up from carrying this all out at the roadside.

We would be crawling around the floor, working away, sweating, and then suddenly there would be a power cut (a fortnightly occurrence). It was so stressful, but we always got through it. I would stick some music on and just dance and sing my way through the surgery, determined that if I was going to have to do it in this weird set-up, I would at least do it my way!

As always, Malaka's incredible improvising skills came in handy, and he got stuck into finding ways to make life here easier for us and the dogs, at little or no cost.

He got hold of some old tyres of different sizes and cut them in half, put a blanket in, and *voilà*, we had dog beds. The dogs loved them and would happily hop in and out of them, scrabbling around to rearrange the blankets because, let's face it, no person ever puts the blanket in quite the way the dog wants it, do they?

Another day I was bemoaning the lack of buster collars for post ops (better known as 'cones of shame' to most people), so Malaka went off and did some research, and came back with an alternative. Turns out a towel wrapped into a sausage shape and taped around a dog's neck will do exactly the same trick. He was always looking at how we could save money in practical, sensible ways.

I was continuing to look for ways myself too, and had begun to occasionally use superglue as an alternative for surgical glue when the dog was under anaesthetic. There is very little difference in the two, other than the fact superglue will sting a little, but if the dog is unconscious, they obviously aren't awake to feel it. It is not something I routinely use, but in the tightest times a dab of superglue was preferable over a surgical glue we couldn't afford. I would never advocate vets using this in general circumstances, and given the choice, the medically correct one is obviously the right one, but we are a charity, and I needed to find ways not to be wasteful.

I hired a local, older man to look after the building and work on the garden. I took to calling him Uncle, a respectful term for your elders here, and it has now stuck. I was determined to make sure there was a lovely, homely area for the dogs who were living there, either permanently, or temporarily, and he did a great job of that, as well as taking on lots of DIY tasks.

Our new clinic was just up the road from Dr Nuwan's place, and when we told him we were opening, he said he would close his and join us. I didn't want him to feel as though he had to, but he said he would actually prefer to consult for us. So he joined us full time for a while, then reduced his hours down so that he could enjoy life a bit more. He has been a huge asset to WECare and really helpful in navigating so many potential pitfalls. It gave me that extra reassurance to have him on the team.

• CHAPTER THIRTEEN •

CALAMITY GEORGE
AND FRIENDS

The first dog I treated in the new clinic was called Polly. She was an adult dog who had been living under a kind of veranda at the side of the road. She had come in with a traumatic amputation – almost half her leg already off – but we needed to take it a bit higher, as there was still bone sticking out.

While she was with us, though, the veranda collapsed. It was such a relief she had been at the clinic, as otherwise there was a good chance she would have been underneath it sleeping when it fell.

I was already in two minds about returning her to the street now she was down to three legs and that decided it for me. That rickety veranda had been her home, so I wouldn't have felt she was being returned to the area she was used to with the veranda gone, and it could have been quite disorientating for her. Her general territory would have been the same, but not quite right.

She had also been with us for a while, and I couldn't guarantee that lots of her territory hadn't been taken over. As a tripod – as our three-legged friends affectionately get called – it was going to be harder for her to reassert herself. So in the end she carried on hanging out with Belle and the others in the garden.

As I now had so much more space, I was less stressed about finding ways to get the dogs back to their original homes, or up for adoption, but equally, I was aware that I didn't want a spiralling cost just from feeding the dogs daily. So I asked Malaka to keep an ear out in case any potential adopters came up for Polly. I wasn't that hopeful – an adult dog with a missing leg, didn't bode too well for her – but then a friend of Malaka's in the village said he would take her. Double result! A new home for Polly, and not far from us, so we could pop in and see her regularly. The ideal outcome for us really.

If there was ever a dog who needed our help, it was Calamity George.

I knew George from my early days in Sri Lanka, having neutered him as a puppy. But then he got papillomavirus – or, put more simply, warts.

I decided to do this really cool surgery (is it only vets who would ever think a certain surgery was cool?) where you autotransplant the wart back into the dog and it effectively acts as a vaccination. That way I wasn't just removing the wart, but making sure they wouldn't reappear.

But in 0.01 per cent of cases it can become cancerous. And of course, being George's luck, he was that 0.01 per cent.

We had to then treat the cancer by surgical removal. That worked but it had knocked his immune system in the process, and his skin went into an awful red raw state, and he developed mange as his defences were so down that the Demodex just went to town. There was nothing for it but to let him live at the clinic for a while, as he recovered. Not that anyone was complaining – we all loved him. He was a real lively character, lovely to all the people and the dogs.

Finally, we felt he was all fixed up and could go back to his life on the street. But the next day he reappeared to see everyone!

After that, he would merrily carry on with his own life, but always with one eye on the clinic and what was happening there. Sometimes he would come for breakfast and sit outside the gate howling until someone let him in. There was nothing wrong with him, he would just be back for a bit of food or some fussing.

If he spotted any of us walking down to the local rice shop for lunch he would fall into line and accompany us, or sometimes he would walk one of the staff home, as though making sure they got there safely.

I always used to say we needed to put a camera on him and watch as he went everywhere and busied himself with everyone. 'The Life of George' would have made a great film!

We talk about people being guardians of the dogs, but it was as though he had appointed himself guardian of the clinic. He had become a real integral part of WECare.

Another early arrivee at the clinic, who has been with us ever since, was Eddie. We picked him up at a CNVR in Niwella. It was the first CNVR where we had pushed through for five days in a row. Intense, but rewarding.

Eddie had arrived for neutering looking pretty mangey, and blind as a bat. Other than his eyesight, I couldn't find much else wrong with him, but I didn't feel I could put him back on the street. I didn't know how long he had survived without sight, but I felt he was really lucky to be alive. There are enough dangers for a fully functional dog to deal with, and it felt he wouldn't stand a chance. I was sure he would be in an RTA within weeks of going back on the street. Equally, he was still capable of some quality of life so I wasn't about to put him to sleep, and I had all this space at the clinic now, right? It didn't seem like a big deal to take him back and have him living there long term.

So Eddie became the next WECare clinic resident, and quickly recovered from the mange, growing a shaggy, black, tan and white coat, while generally getting spoilt.

He goes through phases of treating different bits of the clinic as his home, so whether it is a yard out back, or by the bushes, that is where he will be found. When it is really sunny we put up a parasol for him so he can get shade, and when it is raining he hasn't a clue what to do so just sits there waiting for someone to rescue him! The only place he doesn't like being is indoors.

Eddie is so tolerant, even of the puppies. Any new puppy tends to go over and annoy him, and as he can't see them coming it would be understandable if he was nasty to them, but he's not. He tolerates them bowling over to him and trying to nibble his ears, and just grumbles if they get too annoying. He is basically living out his days and enjoying life. What more can anyone ask for?

One of those early pups was Tootsy Bear – or Tuts for short. She was found at just eight weeks old with the most awful skin. It was just before we had moved into the clinic, so Malaka took her into his home and began her treatment there. Lovely black and tan fur started growing on her, along with four white paws and a tail tip. She struggled a bit with calcium deficiency, but we got that sorted, and when the clinic was up and running, she moved there while finishing her recovery.

In theory she should have been an easy one to get adopted once she was recovered, but it wasn't the case. She has a funny, skittish character, and can be like a shy teenager, which I don't really understand given she has lived a happy life with us from such a young age.

Some days she will bark at you and keep her distance, almost warily, while other times she is running over for cuddles and interested in whatever you are up to. She always knows we are there to help her though, and will come over when in need. Once she had a fishbone stuck in her mouth and she came and lay on my feet on the steps and opened her mouth. I pulled it out, and she bounced back up and on with life. I'm glad she knows she can trust us, I just wish she would be more chilled.

As she has got older she has been great for mothering the puppies and really looks after them.

My absolute favourite of the early arrivals at the new clinic, though, was Ticky. Ticky really was my boy.

I had left the clinic for the day and was heading down the road on my scooter, when the local pharmacist flagged me down. He has always been very supportive of the work we do, and he waved down the road and said there was a dog there that looked as though it was hurt.

I headed down and spotted this poor brown and white dog dragging himself around in the middle of the road with buses whizzing by. He was pulling himself along with his front paws, his bum dragging on the ground and his back legs clearly not working.

I tried to approach him, assuming it would be quite straightforward – he surely couldn't move that quickly, could he? But I think he was already quite freaked out, and as I got closer he dragged himself off at a surprising speed. At a guess he probably hadn't had the best recent treatment from humans, and was determined to keep his distance.

I tried a few times, but it was pretty stressful as the last thing

I wanted to do was chase him into oncoming traffic. He was in a safe position at the side of the road by now, watching me cautiously, so I went back and got Malaka. Bless Malaka, it was another one of those times where he worked some real magic, just talking to the dog and patiently moving closer, until finally, with the help of some food, he managed to get Ticky on to a lead and back to the clinic for assessment.

The most likely explanation was that he had been hit by a car or a tuk-tuk and paralysed, but the fact he could actually move at some speed made me wonder how long he had been surviving in that state. Imagine that. As if the street dogs don't have a hard enough time getting by already, he had been getting by with the use of only two legs.

As well as the physical injuries he was absolutely covered in lice and ticks. I'd never seen so many on a dog until this point, it was pretty horrendous – and hence the unoriginal name! But once we vaccinated him and tackled those, and he got over his initial fear, he turned out to be the happiest little chap. He was about eighteen months old, with these big ears and really sweet nature. A real handsome boy, and I fell madly in love with him.

His bowel and bladder movement was unaffected, but we needed to get stuck into sorting his legs. We spent a lot of time working with him through intensive physio, and slowly but surely his back legs started to work again. We also did hydrotherapy – like physio, but in the sea – which he hated, but before long he started getting movement back, and began to totter around on all four legs, getting steadier by the day.

Soon he was out in the garden, passing his days playing and chilling with Polly, Belle, Eddie and Tootsy Bear, who was his absolute best friend. She might have been a bit hot and cold with people and other dogs, but not Ticky. Those two were real besties.

In theory, he was up for adoption, but he was so at home in the clinic and, being honest, he was such a favourite of mine, that I figured he would just stay with us long term. We never had a conversation about each dog at that stage, it was just that we had never anticipated having so many, but if it made sense for them to stay and they wanted to, they just did!

My buddy Mali, the oldest street dog I knew, made use of the clinic a couple of times too in the early days, thanks to maggots getting into his ears. I could always tell when something was wrong, and would just pull alongside him in the tuk-tuk, tell him to hop in, and up he would jump.

He was a bit of a different dog when he was in the clinic, more like a pet. He was a bit needy, but so ridiculously well behaved. He was this street dog with manners. I would put his bowl of rice out and he would be sat there with his tail going mad, but he wouldn't move to eat until you told him he could. How he learnt to behave like that, I have no idea!

Eddie and Mali would hang out a lot together, two old boys just chilling out in the sun. I think Mali saw it that when he came to the clinic it was more like he was going on holiday for a change of scene, then, when he was ready, he would go back to his home on the street. He is like a puppy in an old dude's body. I love him so much.

Mali was keeping up his holidays away from his street home by going somewhere else too, although I never found out where. Every now and then, as he had done ever since the early days when I met him and was trying to sort his skin, he would disappear off for a couple of weeks at a time. I hated it, as the older he got, and the longer I had known him, the more attached I had got to him, and the idea of any harm coming to him broke my heart. I would worry he was dead, and then he would reappear – and, can you believe it, two years in a row after one of his long trips away, he rocked back up as though nothing had changed on my birthday! I was so relieved, it was like he was giving me a present of his presence.

CHAPTER FOURTEEN

RECOGNITION AND LOSS

A letter arrived through the post, from the then prime minister, David Cameron.

'Dear Janey,

Congratulations! I am delighted to be recognising you as a UK Point of Light. UK Point of Light recognises outstanding individual volunteers who are doing extraordinary things in the service of others.

I believe it is my duty as prime minister to hold up examples of great volunteering and service as an inspiration to others.

On behalf of the whole country, I hope this Point of Light Award can be a small way of saying thank you.'

Wowzers!

It turned out that each weekday the prime minister recognises someone who is making a difference in their community and presents them with a PoL Award. I've no idea if someone nominated me or how he came across the work I was doing, but it was a pretty awesome way to start the day. Apparently I was the first vet to be given a PoL, and it was lovely to receive the recognition. Sometimes I can feel a bit separated from the rest of the world, with my head down beavering away, surrounded by dogs, only stopping to criticise myself for what I haven't yet managed to do. So moments like this are great at getting me to look up, take stock, and realise the positives of what I have actually achieved. It was a nice little touch, so thanks, Mr C.

Then my work with WECare was recognised by both my school and university, which was amazing.

Nottingham University invited me back to receive an Alumni Laureate Award, which given just how many people they have to choose from, made me feel super honoured. While I might have struggled with my time there on a personal level, the teaching was fantastic, as was the support some of the lecturers and fellow graduates have given me since, so it was nice that the university saw I had put all my training to good use.

My pride only grew as I watched the other people there to collect awards as they had all made the most amazing contributions to society, and achieved so much.

I was chatting to one gentleman, Sir Nigel Sherlock, who had been key in improving investment into the north-east of England, and was the lead fundraiser for Sage Gateshead, the famous concert venue right on the River Tyne. As we were chatting we realised we had also gone to the same school, but fifty years apart. Despite the age gap, we found we had loads in common, and I was really chuffed to be receiving an award alongside someone like him.

Barnard Castle School asked me to go back and talk to the students and parents as part of Speech Day. I remembered finding the speeches a bit boring and overly serious when I was a teenager, so I was determined to make mine a lot more informal and chatty. Sometimes it can be hard for students to relate to older guests, but I was hoping they would see me as still relatively young and that I could appeal in a 'well if she can do it, so can I' kind of way.

I loved going back to my old school. It brought back so many happy memories as the school really shaped who I am. But as I waited my turn, I was looking at the girls thinking that although they were only eighteen, they were all wearing so much make-up, and looked about twenty-five, and so much more ahead of their years. I ended up talking about shows like *Love Island*, and saying, 'You don't have to conform to fit in with rubbish like that. Be yourselves, and don't be afraid to show your brains.'

Afterwards the teachers were really complimentary, and said, 'Thank god you said that, as they won't listen to us.'

Who knows if they did, but I tried. Maybe one day one of them will come out and volunteer at WECare with me!

Back before those school and university revisits had happened, though, incredibly I was contacted by the *Daily Mirror* to say I had been nominated for UK Vet of the Year in their Animal Heroes Awards. I've no idea who was responsible for putting me forward – I suspect my mum, although she has always maintained her innocence.

I wasn't sure if I would have time to fly back, and could see I was up against the President of the British Veterinary Association

(BVA) so figured I stood no chance, but they were so persuasive that I slotted in a quick three-day trip. I'd just celebrated my twenty-eighth birthday, so was feeling all positive, and then landing in London I met up with my brother-in-law who was coming as my date and we went straight to the awards. It was a brilliant, glitzy night in London's Grosvenor House Hotel, and was run by the *Mirror* and the RSPCA.

It was lovely to be surrounded by so many people who care about animals, and hear their stories. Then suddenly host Amanda Holden was running through the nominations for Vet of the Year. I was sure there was no way I was going to beat the BVA boss, as he is basically the top dog in the vet business, but before I knew it she was reading my name out. I had the widest ever grin on my face as I floated up to the stage. Move over, everyone, I've bloody made it. This was my Oscar moment!

Amanda asked me how I felt, clearly hoping for a short speech. But nope, I took inspiration from Gwyneth Paltrow and wasn't going to let my moment pass, and any chance of playing it cool went straight out of the window. I didn't want to stop talking in case there was anything I forgot to say, so I told the audience everything I could about our adventure so far, how we were raising money, ways they could help, my hopes for the future … they got the whole lot.

Afterwards I was intent on mingling with the celebrities. I love celebrity news and it doesn't matter that I have been away from the UK for five years, keeping up to date on all the latest gossip has continued to be a lifeline to me. When I have had an emotionally draining or particularly traumatic day there is nothing I like more than settling into bed and reading the cheeky, light, entertainment news. So it was awesome to be chatting away to Alesha Dixon, Ferne McCann and Laura Whitmore, all of whom were lovely and so supportive of what we were doing. I was impressed as they didn't have to listen and ask questions of someone like me, but they took the time to do so. I was eyeing Paul O'Grady from afar, as he was there to get an award for Outstanding Contribution, but I was too nervous to go and say hi!

It goes without saying that I couldn't be back in the UK and not go and see my beloved Finn. He had now moved from Alex's house to live with my mum, and I knew he was happy there, but I missed him so much. Even though I knew if he had been able to understand where I was he would absolutely have given me his approval, I still hated having left him behind.

So I jumped on the train the morning after the awards, and headed up to Mum's to see him for twenty-four hours. I was floating along on a high, feeling all cruisy and positive about life, after my birthday and the award. Life was good.

Finn went crazy, jumping all over the place and panting as I sat trying to cuddle him, laughing. He didn't leave my side for my brief visit, and we went for a final walk on the fell just before I had to leave to get my flight.

It felt so right to be back there with him, that as I walked I was hit by a real longing to move home. I'd left my boy for so long already, was it time I came back to him? He was still only eleven so we had a good few years together ahead of us, but we'd already missed out on so much. He was the one thing that really could make me leave Sri Lanka. There was a string tying us together that couldn't be broken, despite all the mileage between us, and the poor pup had put up with me abandoning him for so long already.

Just then I realised Finn was pulling up a bit, and looked as though each step was causing him pain. That wasn't like him at all, and eventually I had to carry him home.

Of course I was worried, but I also knew he suffered from chronic pancreatitis, which means he would get bouts of sickness and pain thanks to his pancreas getting inflamed, so I thought it might just be a flare-up of that. Besides, I had been paying for him to get scanned by the top ultrasound specialist in the North and get his bloods tested every six months, so I was confident that anything else would have been picked up during that. I gave him some pain relief, along with strict instructions for Mum about his care, then headed off.

Landing in Sri Lanka, I got a call to say he wasn't doing so well. Then two hours later he was reportedly fine again. But the next day, 10 September, he collapsed and Mum rushed him straight to my best friend Laura, who is also a vet. She found a tumour on his spleen, which was bleeding, and he needed a splenectomy (removal of his spleen) and a blood transfusion. Tragically it seemed the cancer had also spread to his liver and lungs.

I couldn't understand it. This was Finny, my boy, who had seemed absolutely fine just days before. There had to be a way to fix him.

I spent all night on the phone trying to sort what I could. It was a horrible shock for Laura too, as we had lived together at university with her dogs and Finn, so he was her dog too in a way. I am sure she felt hideous, but I was glad she was able to take on his care.

I flew home. It was like I had been on an absolute high, loving the way my life was going, and riding the encouraging wave of the award. And then, suddenly, everything I based myself on was being pulled from under me. The best moment of my life had been followed by the worst.

Back in the UK I put all my time and energy into Finn. For two weeks I spent every moment with him, going for walks when he felt up to it, and snuggling in bed with him when he didn't. It was lovely in a way, to spend time that was so completely just about making him happy.

I was due to fly back to Sri Lanka for an intense CNVR clinic, which was being sponsored by a £17,000 donation from Dogs Trust. It was a big deal, and I knew I really should be there. But I didn't want to leave Finn, so I was torn. It was such a tough decision to make.

I had referred him to a specialist at Edinburgh University who thought he would be okay for another six weeks, and the airline wouldn't let me switch flights, so in the end I decided to go, and then return to the UK as soon as possible.

It wasn't to be. Two days after I went back to Sri Lanka, on 30 September, my Finn was put to sleep. I was on Skype while it happened, so that I could feel I was there for him and reassure him, but watching this beautiful boy's life being cut short was the saddest moment of my whole existence.

I did not handle it well at all. I felt like my child had died and I couldn't function. At first I was consumed with anger. I resented all the other dogs who had taken up the time I should have spent with Finn. I'd sacrificed my last couple of years with him for these dogs on the other side of the world that I hadn't even known at the time. And why were they still alive, when he had died?

Back in Sri Lanka I went straight into a CNVR after five days with pretty much no sleep. 'I don't care about any of you,' I thought bitterly in my head, looking at all the dogs rounded up. I felt like I had no love or compassion to give them that day, as they were the lucky ones – they were still alive.

Then I had a work stint booked in Dubai, but things were no better there. I was judging every owner in my head and just felt so hard done by. 'I don't think you care enough about your dog, so why do you deserve him? I loved Finn more than the world itself, and I lost him. It's not fair.'

This lovely couple brought their dog into the clinic, really worried as he had splenic tumours like Finn, but whereas Finn's were malignant, I was able to break the news to this couple that their dog's were benign – harmless. Even though I knew it was wrong, rather than being happy for them I was bitter.

And then I started blaming myself. I had left him when he

needed me. I'd been really selfish coming out here to follow my own dream. What kind of vet was I, that I could save all these other dogs and not my own? Why hadn't I prevented this, and protected him the way I was meant to? It was hard to be a good vet at that time, when I felt so disillusioned. People think I should be tough as a vet, that I have seen it all, but in a way that made it worse. I know all about animal medical care, and yet it still happened. It blew my mind.

But there was no option but to plough on, and over time, while I didn't get over Finn – and never will – I got past that awful negative mindset. Of course it wasn't these other poor dogs' faults that Finn had died, and nor was it mine. In my rational moments, I knew that even the best vet in the world couldn't have saved him.

Eventually I decided that maybe the Vet of the Year award was tied in with his death. They had happened so close to each other that maybe that was Finn's way of letting me know I was free to carry on, and that is what he wanted: 'Go on, you are doing a good thing. You are sorted now, so keep doing it.'

I don't know. That might sound daft to other people, but to me it felt like the timing was too perfect to ignore. Finn would be proud if I carried on and helped hundreds more animals, so that was what I vowed to do.

CHAPTER FIFTEEN

THE CLINIC IS FAMOUS!

We pushed on, now treating dozens of dogs each day, but the financial situation was getting desperate. Despite having our own building, it was still effectively an empty shell. I simply didn't have the money to kit it out. I was operating on the floor with the most basic of equipment, one functioning sink, constantly sweating without air conditioning, and just about able to pay my basic staff. The one plus point was I was starting to get longer-term volunteer vets, including my first one who came out for six months, and threw herself into the life here alongside me. She accepted the set-up for what it was, never complaining, and for that alone I was super thankful.

In the meantime I had filmed a short documentary with a friend that he pitched for a slot on BBC North East and Cumbria called *Inside Out*. It was for a ten-minute slot that focuses on surprising real-life stories, and summarised what WECare does and how we were getting on. I felt a bit daft talking to the camera as my friend followed me around, as I had never done anything like that before, and had no idea how I would come across to any viewers. But ultimately I didn't know when or if it would be aired, so I kind of put it out of my mind.

Then one morning in January 2017 I woke up to all these notifications on social media, and about a thousand new emails. Turns out a snippet of the show had been released to *BBC News* who had posted it online, and it was the most watched news on the site that day – more than Trump's inauguration. My initial reaction was, 'WTF!' It was amazing, but completely overwhelming. Then BBC Three pulled together a longer version of it for their *Amazing Humans* series.

Once it had gone online, things really took off, it kept getting shared around the Internet and across the world. It was unexpected and exciting to see how many people were learning about our existence, but it was also a real rollercoaster from then on in (in case life hadn't been crazy enough out here before now).

Viewers were really keen to know how to donate, so we were getting the info out there as widely as possible on social media, and by replying to emails, then I'd look at WECare's account and see all these lovely donations coming in. Just in time is all I can say. It was such a relief to know that the financial pressure would ease, for a bit at least.

But then I'd look online at an article someone had written about the show, and although 99 per cent of the readers' comments underneath were positive, I'd zoom in on the negative ones, and my mood would plummet.

One minute I'd open my emails and find the sweetest messages from people all over the world who had taken the time to send over their thoughts, and I'd feel lifted up, only to go on social media, see some really vile abuse, and I'd be spiralling down again.

You have to wonder why someone would hate a story like mine, but some of the stuff people wrote was really shocking. I was called 'disgusting', with one woman even saying I should be euthanised. It really rocked me.

When I'd read about celebs complaining about being trolled in the past, I'd always just thought, 'Get over it, it's silly harmless stuff.' I can promise you, I will never say that again! When it happens to you, it feels like such a horrible, personal attack. I wasn't prepared for it in the slightest. Even though you know they don't know you and are just going on the attack as they are nasty people with too much time on their hands, it doesn't change how you feel at that moment.

Besides, as far as I was concerned the documentary was so positive about everything that I couldn't believe people were able to find something negative in it, and take exception to it.

Some amazing coverage appeared about us in the UK press, and the BBC told us they had never received such an incredible response to a documentary of that type. Word continued to spread, and before we knew it the viewing figures had reached an immense thirty-two million.

But the negative comments continued, and I haven't had media training and I'm not tough skinned, so I felt like I couldn't get past it. Back home I might have fared better. I would have had my friends and family around me, telling me, 'It's bullshit, ignore it, now let's go out!' but here there aren't those people to give you a reality check. In fact, the opposite happens – everything is magnified and becomes more of a drama.

Frustratingly, it wasn't helped by three articles written by me appearing in *Vet Times* at the same time. I had written them eighteen months before when I had been looking for a way to raise extra funds (they pay £250 an article) but they weren't published until this point. I'd written about the street dogs and their care (or lack of) within six months of arriving in the country and my opinions and observations had changed a bit since then. There wasn't anything factually wrong in the articles, but I perhaps hadn't developed as much of an understanding of the situation as I had by the time they were published. While I had run them past three local vets and a Sri Lankan family who all said there was nothing offensive in them, that wasn't the general opinion once they were published.

Add that to the backlash from the documentary, and the reaction from some parts of the Sri Lankan veterinary community was brutal. They didn't like that I was highlighting that these street dogs were getting ignored, and went to town on me.

One guy had a letter published in the *Vet Times* that said I'd disrespected the profession and should be struck off. It is a professional publication read by every vet in the UK so that was incredibly humiliating.

I felt burnt, broken-hearted and traumatised, and flew to Dubai in tears for an escape and to work out how to cope with it all. I felt like I had given up my life in the UK to make this work, and dealt with hurdle after hurdle, and all I was getting for it was one kick in the teeth, followed by another. I was still fragile after losing Finn, and didn't see how I was going to get through this.

I stayed with a friend and closed myself off from all the negativity, and gave myself the breathing space to sit back and focus on all the amazing stuff that was coming out of the documentary. I sat and watched the donations going up, reread the amazing messages – for every negative comment, I'd had a thousand positive ones – and reminded myself that it wasn't about me, it was about the dogs. There was no way I could let some small-minded idiots stop me from doing what I knew was the right thing. This was about Belle, George, Ralphie, Mali, and the thousands of others like them. The more I pulled my mind back to the bigger picture of what needed to be done, the better I felt. It was time I got myself back to Sri Lanka, and put that extra money to good use.

Top: Jo – my superstar practice manager. No job was too challenging or too small for her. I couldn't have managed without her.

Bottom: Vinura's enthusiasm was so inspiring for me and all the volunteers. We were devasted when he was killed in a motorbike accident. He will always be an important part of WECare.

Top: It's not just dogs we treat at the clinic – I've treated cows, cats, birds, bats, lizards, a goat, and in this case a monkey.

Bottom: Aureliya was the first cat we treated – she came in after someone spotted her with an injured leg.

Top: My contact with the dogs has helped to teach the locals that there is no need to be afraid of the street dogs.

Bottom: Lucy suffered horrendous injuries after she was attacked by a wild boar. I've no doubt she would have been put to sleep in the UK but she recovered remarkably well.

Top left: Barry came to us with a broken leg but soon became a bit of a mystery after he was suddenly paralysed from the neck down – luckily he has since recovered.

Top right: Dinush was Jo's landlord and didn't like dogs one bit at the start, but soon he fell in love with them and the dogs living with Jo had a second home to go to!

Bottom: Benji was a mangey little pup who was dumped on my doorstep. I had intentions of rehoming him but his sweet personality got under my skin and I was too attached to him to give him up.

Top: Bonnie was found by Jo at a bus station having lost part of her leg. She adapted to having three legs incredibly well and became best friends with fellow tripod Lucky.

Bottom: Adoption days have been a brilliant way of allowing the community to interact with the dogs and bring out the animal lovers in the area.

Top: Using the ocean on our doorstep is a great way of being able to treat the dogs with techniques like hydrotherapy without the need for an expensive pool.

Bottom: The clinic featured on Ben Fogle's TV series 'New Lives in the Wild' – it was an amazing way to show the world all the work the clinic is doing and we raised a lot of money afterwards.

Top: Children often ask me questions about the dogs so we began doing impromptu visits at schools. Here's Jo teaching them understand the best way to approach the dogs.

Bottom: Happy, healthy dogs relaxing on the beach.

Top: Beautiful Belle helped me as much as I helped her.
Her resilience and positive outlook could teach most
people a thing or two about the best way to live.

Donations kept coming in over the next few months, and in the end the documentary raised around £70,000 in total for us, which was amazing. We decided to put a large portion of it towards bringing in equipment that we desperately needed. And I'm not just talking about medical equipment, but even such basics as desks and a microwave.

One lovely man called Fred Crook got in touch with me after watching the documentary to say he was the boss of a shipping company called The Courier Company, and if we wanted to fill a container, they would ship it to us for free. Well, we weren't going to turn that down, were we?

We started sourcing everything from tables and sinks, to air conditioning, operating tables and computers. It might sound surprising that we looked for electronics in the UK, but despite the fact that life is generally way cheaper out here, anything electric, such as washing machines, printers, hoovers etc., all cost way more and there isn't really a second-hand market for them, as people use them until they have completely given up.

So we were able to make use of two vital things in the UK to fill the container – the second-hand market through places such as Gumtree, where we could get our hands on a washing machine for £50, rather than £500, and also benefit from items donated by companies.

We sourced all the materials to build kennels out the back of the building. I wanted somewhere for dogs who needed a bit more space, but who also weren't yet ready to mix with the dogs in the garden. Whenever a dog comes into the clinic, unless we know all their vaccinations are up to date, they are kept separated from other dogs just as a matter of course for two weeks, and the kennels would make this much easier. I'd had quotes from steel workers in Sri Lanka, but the price difference was huge. Being able to build those was going to be a real asset to the clinic, so into the container those materials went too.

The day that container arrived was such a high point. I remember the total excitement as we unloaded it. Twenty Christmases in one go.

I was still getting some out-of-date meds, as having a bit of money didn't suddenly mean I was going to splash the cash. We had scrimped and saved every step of this journey, so I wanted to continue being as careful. We added suture material to the list of what we would accept, after a cardiac surgeon in the UK told me that if you can stretch it, and it doesn't snap, then it is fine to use, even if it is five years out of date. I used my discretion and put that information to use, but I have also put a two-year limit on everything, just so I have a cut-off point.

We didn't just get materials from vet suppliers either, but I was able to get some equipment from human medicine. Some of the instruments such as scissors or clamps cross over between the two jobs, but are regarded as single use in human medicine. It is honestly one of the most wasteful industries on the planet. We have the means to sterilise this equipment with autoclaves, and yet whether for ease or paranoia that it won't be cleaned properly, they are binned every time. There must be literally millions of these pieces of equipment in landfill. We cannot afford to do that in the animal industry, so I started offering to take this equipment off people's hands, which then saved further funds.

There were other incredible things that happened after the documentary too, such as the arrival of my superstar practice manager, Jo Armitage. Jo was a Brit who had been backpacking through Sri Lanka and fallen in love with the country, but felt frustrated at the state of the dogs. She had moved on to New Zealand by the time she saw the documentary and had got in touch to see if there was any way she could come back and work for us. A few months and life changes later, she came to join us, and proved to be an absolute godsend. The clinic was still in this insanely basic state, with us operating on floors, and making do with anything we could. She didn't bat an eyelid, and got stuck in doing everything from sourcing equipment, to helping set up CNVRs, clearing up dog shit, to comforting upset owners. No job was too challenging for Jo, or beneath her, and she did whatever was needed, working every available hour. She was brilliantly personable and would play a great good cop to my bad cop when it came to handling the staff. She's no walkover, though, and somehow people found they were doing exactly as she wanted, without realising how it happened. Oh, and she is also fearless and a natural with dogs. While she had never worked as a practice manager before, she slotted into the role perfectly.

Basically things began running much more smoothly with her arrival, and it really allowed me to return my focus to the animals and the future of WECare.

I was also able to start hiring, and took on a few younger guys such as Babi and Sachira who I already knew from the village as their families had previously helped out with dogs, so I knew they were genuinely interested.

Doctor Nuwan's nephew, Vinura, also began working with us as a volunteer. He had just turned seventeen, and I loved him from day one. He turned up with this thick head of hair, and big sunny smile on his face. I instantly knew he was going to be a huge asset to WECare, as he was a complete natural with the dogs, but he also radiated positive energy.

It wasn't long before we couldn't keep him away from the place. He would come in six days a week, assisting with everything from cleaning out kennels, to comforting the dogs during treatment.

We had turned the container into a flat, as we wanted someone to be at the clinic twenty-four hours a day, and as Vinura's family lived about an hour away, this was perfect for him. He would live there during the week, so that he could be the first person up with the dogs in the morning, and the last person chilling with them, giving them cuddles while he watched films, until eleven p.m. at night.

I also had a great team of nurses start to join me. Most were short-term volunteers – or vollies as we call them – although I have had one, Emily Dorner, who came out indefinitely, and has been an absolute godsend.

The only problem was that it had just been Malaka, Chaminda and me for so long (plus DN at times) that Malaka didn't take kindly to the new people. He found it difficult to adapt to them, and was really stubborn about the change. He was also such a hard worker that it would wind him up to the point of tears if he didn't think other people were working as hard as they should. But I was determined to increase the number of staff, as if we wanted to help more dogs, it was the only way, and over time Malaka slowly began to accept it was the way forward.

The whole experience of taking part in the documentary was incredible for the charity, and if I was to do everything over, I'd still go through with it, as it basically allowed the charity to grow and develop in the way it has – therefore saving hundreds more dogs. But it did make me realise that I am more fragile than I sometimes will admit to myself. Everything about WECare is really personal, it is my life's work, and I care so deeply about it, that if someone slags it off, or takes issue with it, I really take it to heart.

Basically the moral of this chapter is, if you don't like anything you read in this book, don't tell me, just message me lovely amazing things, as you don't want to be responsible for breaking me, right?

CHAPTER SIXTEEN

IT'S NOT JUST DOGS, DOGS, DOGS ...

'Hi there, a whole gang of monkeys have just turned on one of their own, and he has been bitten, scratched, and knocked to the ground unconscious. Can you help?'

Street dogs are obviously our main priority here, but I am never going to say no to any other animal in real need. I have a duty of care as a vet, which means that any creature who needs health-care treatment is going to receive it, no matter how bizarre it might sound. But I've got to say, monkeys are not the easiest.

They are really common in Sri Lanka, especially the brown/grey-coloured Toque Macaque. Most days they can be spotted bouncing through the trees, or climbing across the roofs or balconies of houses. They are confident, and have been known to dash into houses to steal food, but they rarely come into actual contact with humans. The locals aren't generally big fans and see them as a bit of a nuisance, and true enough they can seem like a law unto themselves.

Monkeys are brought in to us for any number of reasons, such as head trauma caused by RTAs, or falling off power lines. This particular one was brought to us as he had been attacked by other monkeys for a reason we will never know. Monkeys have really sharp teeth and they can inflict some serious damage if they want to. They are also quite brutal animals when in a pack, so if they turn on one monkey en masse, that one doesn't stand a chance.

The people who had called had managed to pick the injured monkey up in a bag while he was still unconscious, and bring him in. But by the time I opened the bag he had most definitely come round. Without warning he sprung around the treatment room, bouncing off the walls, as we all desperately tried to catch him again. He had some really bad gashes, potential breaks, and was in a highly distressed state.

Knowing it is the rest of his troop who were responsible for the damage made it particularly hard when thinking of this little guy's future, as he couldn't be introduced back to his old pack, or they would attack again, but neither are monkeys solitary creatures.

Regardless of that, while I am not an expert in monkey veterinary science, I will always give it my best shot. Unfortunately, shock is a really big thing with these guys. Not like an 'oh you made me jump' shock, but shock as a clinical syndrome, where blood pressure drops, and there is a shortage of oxygen to the vital organs.

Monkeys are brought to us never having been handled by a human before, and the clinical environment is completely alien to them, so it is terrifying. Add that to the fact they are often critical cases, and even though we will try and keep the situation as calm and simple as possible, a lot of the time, as happened to this poor wee guy, the shock kills them before I've had a chance to treat them.

Cats are the second most common animal that we take in after dogs – everything from stray kittens who are too small to be without their mum, to cats injured by RTAs. While lots of them can be really chilled – weirdly more chilled than the cats in Dubai and the UK – those that aren't are harder to deal with than dogs, as they are ridiculously fast, and have more they can attack you with. When it comes to dogs, once you take away the potential weapon of their jaw, with a muzzle, they tend to just accept the situation. A cat, however, has its mouth and four claw-filled paws to do battle with, and unlike a dog they rarely give you warning nips, or signs of what is about to come!

We don't often come across injured cats ourselves, I guess as they tend to be harder to spot, and will hide themselves away when hurt. So most of them have been brought in by a caring passerby who has spotted them, or an owner. Lots of cats have homes here, as while street dogs are seen by some as dirty and diseased, cats are viewed as cuter and cleaner. Our first cat was called Aureliya and came in when someone spotted her lying by a nearby shop with a mangled leg. The leg was a lost cause, so we amputated it, then she stayed at my house while she recovered, becoming best friends with a puppy called Oscar, who was also with me at the time. Aureliya was really cute, and Malaka's parents eventually adopted both her and Oscar.

We have also treated cows, birds, bats, lizards and a goat. In theory I have learnt how to deal with every animal at some point in my studies, so can treat them all. But occasionally I'll get an unexpected animal with an even more unexpected problem, and it is a bit like, 'Someone pass me a book, quick!' I've got a small library of books in the clinic for exactly that reason.

Then there are the wild boar, who I can only describe as totally and utterly nuts. Without doubt, they are the animal I find hardest to treat. There is absolutely no chance of making friends with them, and they have a real fight or flight instinct when it comes to people. The adult ones can come up to hip height, but even the piglets can reach your knee, and they are incredibly strong.

I was called out to treat a tiny young one that someone had found paralysed in their garden, but despite that he still had so much power. Several of the locals had him pinned down with a V stick around his neck. At first I thought it was unnecessary, then when I saw his strength and the fact they were just about holding him, I realised it actually worked very well. There was no way he could have been brought into the clinic, and I had to treat him on the spot.

Boar tusks are pretty intimidating, particularly as I have seen first hand the damage they have done to Belle, and the many other boar-attack dogs who have been in for treatment since. But as with all animals, if we get a call-out to an injured boar, or one is brought in and we think there is anything we can do to help, we always will.

Since Belle we have had quite a few dogs who are the victims of those sharp boar weapons – an average of one admission a month. The only thing I will say is, it is rarely the boar who have gone looking for trouble, nor the dogs who have gone looking for boar, but just an unlucky coincidence. The adult boar are very protective of their young, and they spend their time in the long grass, so often a dog sniffing around won't know he is encroaching on their territory until it is too late.

One of these was Lucy, a typical golden-brown street dog from Galle who was brought in by a lady who had found her after she had been attacked by a wild boar. The woman kindly offered to be her guardian if we were able to treat her.

Lucy had a massive hole in her side, and two ruptured Achilles tendons. She needed tendon grafts, which was particularly hard as there was a five-centimetre deficit with one of them. It was tricky surgery, and one of the grafts failed, but the other lasted the distance. She recovered with just a scar on her side to show the damage, as well as being a bit flat hocked.

Her treatment would have cost at least £6,000 in the UK, but most likely wouldn't have even been attempted in the first place. I've no doubt she would have been put to sleep. But for us it is a case of, we don't want to go down that route unless we have exhausted all else, so we will always try all the options first. Make a plan, take a deep breath, and get stuck in.

In the end we didn't send Lucy back to the street with her guardian, as we were worried about any complications with her flat foot, so she stayed on at the clinic. Understandably, Lucy now goes crazy if she realises there is a boar in the vicinity, but when the boar realises there are dogs nearby, they will head on their way.

Only once have we treated a dog who seemed to have been sought out and purposefully attacked. Lassie was tied up outside a house overnight and a boar wandered into the garden and went for her. It seemed out of character for a boar, and I'd never heard of it happening before then.

A bit like with Belle, it got round her side and stuck its tusks in, ripping into her chest, stomach and leg. Normally in the UK you would refer a dog with that kind of damage on to a specialist, but as usual there was no choice, we just had to get on with it. Lassie had to have a thoracotomy – an operation in her chest cavity – as well as fifteen centimetres of gut removed, and a hind limb amputation. It was a massive amount of surgery, and effectively three procedures in one. It would probably have been deemed too much for a dog to go through in the UK, but knowing the resilience of the Sri Lankan dogs we gave it a crack. Sure enough, Lassie pulled through it all and went home, remarkably just two weeks later.

The surgery had mainly been carried out by a volunteer vet who was over at the time, and I was super proud of her for achieving it and saving Lassie's life. But when we put details of the case on our social media, I was shocked by the backlash. Rather than congratulating our vet on the job she had done some people were focused on the fact we were allowing her to go back to a family who had tied the dog up outside. They were questioning why we wouldn't just keep her ourselves, and deemed it cruelty for her to go back. A classic case of judgements made on a Sri Lankan situation, with western eyes.

I'm not a fan of dogs being tied up, but that is more the people who chain them up twenty-four hours a day as guard dogs. For Lassie's owners it was more of a safety concern, to stop the dog wandering off around the main road in the dark. She was on a long chain, had access to water, and in reality spent her night sleeping on her bed. The boar attack was a one-off, so to be honest I think this is more responsible dog ownership than those who let them walk around at night.

I had also seen first hand how the owners rushed Lassie straight to us, visited her every day, and didn't question paying for all her treatment. They were really affected by what had happened, and clearly cared deeply for her. So it does irritate me when people who don't understand the situation here are so quick to write off people who are actually bloody good owners.

CHAPTER SEVENTEEN

UNEXPECTED DANGERS

Life in Sri Lanka just seems all round harder and more extreme, whether you are a human or an animal. At times it feels like there is danger lurking around every corner, and it seems a miracle that these dogs ever survive!

If a dog in the UK sees something interesting and unknown lying on some rubbish, an odd-shaped rock, an abandoned bit of rope, or a swirling leaf, there's usually no danger. Not so in Sri Lanka.

Nope, out here it could be a snare, an explosive left for wild boar, a scorpion, or any number of other creatures capable of inflicting immeasurable pain.

The biggest risk of all for inquisitive dogs, though, is snakes. There are ninety-six different types of snake in Sri Lanka, and while only five of those can kill humans – and generally will only do so if disturbed or cornered – a larger percentage of the snakes can be pretty damaging to dogs.

The undergrowth and bushes the dogs roam through means they are never far away from snakes. Add that to their plain nosy and naive nature, and it makes dogs destined for a fall.

'I'm sure that bit of rope moved,' they think, wandering over to check it out.

'Better give it a shake, to be sure. Oh, it's alive, I am sure it will want to play with me.'

And before you know it, they've got themselves a nasty, poisonous bite.

We see so many snake bites in the clinic, but unfortunately while people do their best and rush the dogs to us, they are often dead on arrival. If they make it in time, we administer an anti-venom injection near the bite site, then put the dog on what is known as a CRI – continuous rate infusion – that keeps meds dripping constantly through an IV line. Then they go on antibiotics and IV fluids. Providing the dog reaches us quickly enough – generally within the hour – that course of treatment can often save the dog's life.

Timing is the most important element, but things such as the size of the dog and where they are bitten can be crucial too. We had one brought in who had eaten a snake, and we tried our best, but sadly the poison was effectively eating him up from the inside.

It isn't always the dogs' fault they have been bitten. Some of the gutsier snakes can view puppies – and more particularly kittens – as easy food. Yet another reason why the youngsters have such low rates of survival past infancy.

I had a great little puppy called Scampi, who used to live with me before we had the hospital. We had picked him up at the roadside, suffering badly with mange and completely hairless. There was a volunteer over at the time who wanted to take him back to the UK, but she didn't, and he just ended up with me. A guy I was dating then always used to complain about the mangey puppy next to me when I collapsed onto the sofa at the end of each day. Okay, in retrospect, maybe he did stink, but tough, that dog was the best cuddler going!

Then we found him this perfect home with a kid who absolutely loved him to bits, and I just felt so pleased, as life was finally complete for Scampi. But then one day he was bitten by a snake, and that was it, the end of poor Scampi.

It was the same with a puppy called Timmy. We rescued him, fixed his leg, and the next thing you know he was killed by a snake.

In my more pessimistic moments, I've wondered whether it is almost like the harder you work to save a dog's life, the more likely it is that something else is going to happen to them. It is almost like the *Final Destination* films. Time is meant to be up for these dogs, and then I come along and intervene. But death, who has decided it is their time, keeps fighting back, and all I can do is delay it a bit. It is like the grim reaper is constantly stalking these poor dogs.

Those are only my thoughts when I'm feeling a bit negative though! The reality is, that is the nature of life in Sri Lanka. Life is not simple for these dogs, and death unfortunately is an everyday risk.

I'm always worried about my dogs with snakes – it is one of the main reasons I have them sleeping indoors at night, as I want to reduce their chances of falling victim to a snake bite.

Of course, snakes can be out in the day too though. One afternoon while I was at home, the dogs were all barking like mad and I looked out to see them gathered around a bush in the corner of my garden. I wandered over, and there was a King Cobra in there with his neck stuck right up, and the hood around his head spread bigger than my hand, hissing like mad.

My heart rate shot up, and I yelled at the dogs to get in

the house. But their interest was overriding any fear they might have had, and they didn't move – until I resorted to the old trick of running in and shaking their food bowls!

Even then it took a minute or so before they came running, and I was freaking out, so scared for them.

Once they were in I locked all the doors – I know, I know, what snake can open *unlocked* doors? – but even with all the windows closed I could still hear its hissing from outside.

I'm not too scared of snakes for myself – if it's my time thanks to a snake bite, then I guess that is how I go! – and I think living out here you have to get used to them. There is definitely a time and a place for them though. I'm not trying to claim I'm tough – if I was in bed and one suddenly crawled through the window and over the cover, yes, I'd be freaking out. When I first arrived and was staying at Talalla Retreat we would get them all the time. We were in a house above the retreat that was pretty much in the jungle – in fact so much so that it was called The Jungle House – and we would have the doors open all the time so all sorts would come in and out. Once my friend was in the bathroom and realised there was a snake hiding in the bin right by the door, and he was panicking that he was trapped. In the end he took a running jump to get past, while we just stood and laughed!

I found a cobra living in the surfboard bag under my bed at one point. He was just curled up chilling in there, who knows how long for. Another time, unfortunately one of my dogs, Stitch, got hold of a rat snake (not poisonous) and had managed to paralyse it. It was there with its head and neck moving, but the rest of its body no longer functioning, and looked terrified, the poor thing. I took advice and in the end had to kill it with a spade. It was horrible, and I was apologising to this snake as I did it, but I couldn't do anything except put it out of its misery.

Then there are monitors. If you haven't seen them before, they are like huge lizards with long necks, tails and claws. Dogs and monitors are a bit more easily matched. You might assume a dog would easily win in a fight, as the monitors are generally ambling along and only have smallish mouths, but in reality they can move fast when they want to, and have a real lethal tail swipe that can cause serious injury to the dog. They occasionally appear in the garden, and we need to keep a close eye out – for the sake of both the monitors and dogs!

But dogs and crocs? That is a different story. In theory the crocodiles – who have been known to grow up to seventeen-feet long on the island – keep themselves out of the way of human society. They stick to the bigger swampy rivers and creeks away from the towns, and in turn people show them respect and don't go and swim through their areas. Occasionally there is a crossover – heavy storms plus high rivers can see crocodiles being swept over the very croc traps laid to stop this happening, and be swept into the sea. Surfing and swimming in the day or two after a storm isn't always advised, for exactly that reason.

Dogs are small enough to be easier prey for crocodiles, and unfortunately I have heard plenty of stories of a dog getting snatched from the beach or a riverbank. And once again, you can guarantee a nosy dog hasn't always made life easy for itself!

I had never heard of any of these dogs surviving, unfortunately, until one day we had a panicked call from a guy in Tangalle, a town about forty minutes along the coast. This man had seen a seven-foot croc hanging around near his home, and had been doing what he could to scare it off. He thought it was gone, when his dog Mischa suddenly stumbled back into the house, with huge wounds all down the sides of her body. It looked like the croc had gone for her, and whether she had wriggled at the right moment, or had fought like a crazy thing, she had managed to get free. I would have loved to have seen the footage of exactly what had happened, because for that girl to have got away alive makes her a total superstar.

The owner had taken Mischa straight to the closest vet who had stitched up the wounds. He wanted to bring her over to us for a look over and a second opinion. I was a bit worried the stitches were quite tight, as I knew she was going to swell up and be in some serious pain over the coming days, but ultimately the vet had done a great job, and saved Mischa's life.

Mischa – or Crocodog as she was nicknamed – was obviously still on a bit of an adrenaline high when she came through our doors, as she couldn't stop grinning as we checked her over! But the poor wee thing had to be carried, as while her legs were fine, every step clearly caused shooting pains down her sides. She had over one hundred stitches holding her together. Of course as well as pain relief we handed the owner lots of antibiotics, as with that many wounds, risk of infection can be quite high, and you never know where the croc's teeth have been before. She has since made a complete recovery and gone back to living life to the full – although hopefully is less inquisitive now.

The other unexpected danger dogs face is the unknown. By that I mean a disease or problem that, despite my best attempts, I just can't identify. It doesn't happen that often, but occasionally I can't diagnose what is wrong, even though it is clear that something is. It is one of the reasons I say I am always learning. There will always be rare illnesses that I haven't come across before, which might be unique to the country or haven't yet been discovered or understood across Asia either. My growing stack of reference books help me out, as do the brilliant set of people I keep in touch with at home. But sometimes I just can't explain something, and that frustrates the hell out of me and, depending on the outcome, can eat me up for months.

One unexpected danger happened to the most gorgeous boy, Barry the singing dog. Barry was brought to us from a hotel in Tangalle, with a broken leg. He was a stunning black, short-haired dog, who looked like he belonged in Egyptian times, but he was far too skinny.

He stayed with us for six weeks with his leg in a cast, while we tried to fatten him up and give him lots of love, attention, and room to heal. I have never met such a vocal dog in my life. He would howl all the time, but not in a distressed way, just in a happy, 'I like the sound of my own voice' kind of a way. We used to say he was singing all the time – even if it was only a good tune in his own head!

He quickly became a firm favourite in the clinic with his quirky, warm personality and his unique vocals, but eventually I knew it was getting close to the time for him to leave. Despite our best efforts he hadn't put on much weight, but he seemed to be eating well, so I was starting to consider castrating him, so he could be on his way. But when I went to assess him that day, he was totally silent. Strange. 'Have you lost your voice, Baz? Sang a bit too much yesterday?'

I was making light of it, but deep down it worried me, as it was such an integral part of his personality. Saying my concerns aloud I thought they sounded daft, so I decided it wasn't anything to worry about, and that I should enjoy the peace instead.

But the next day I was shocked to get to the clinic and find my poor Barry completely paralysed from the neck down. We hurriedly scooped him up on to the table and checked all his reflexes. There were none. Nothing from the neck down got a response, and his gorgeous voice was completely gone. He couldn't pee by himself, and had no interest in eating or drinking. Only his worried eyes, following me as I tried my best to get to the bottom of what had happened, gave any sign that the Barry we knew and loved was still in there.

Eventually it had to be said – there was a high chance he was showing signs of rabies, as paralysis is a common symptom. If that was the case, putting him to sleep was the only option, as dogs do not recover from that, and it would only prolong his agony.

But what if it wasn't that? While we didn't want him to be suffering, none of us could bear to let him go just yet. Who knows, maybe a miraculous recovery could be in store? This was our Barry, and I didn't want to give up on him until I was totally sure.

So I had him moved into isolation in a back room and kept comfortable, while we kept an eye on him. For a few days nothing happened. He didn't seem to deteriorate further, but nor did he get better. I was sure if it wasn't rabies that it was something linked with the neurological system, so in desperation I emailed one of my old neuro lecturers from university. They have always encouraged past students to get in touch with any problems. The lovely lecturer replied suggesting a rare condition called polyradiculoneuritis – paralysis caused by inflammation of the nerves. It is an autoimmune complex condition that can be brought on by several freaky causes, such as raccoon saliva – I don't imagine that could be the cause here. But being really thin was one of the signs. He recommended a really high dose of steroids to treat it and, with nothing to lose, I went for it. Incredibly, it started to work, and suddenly on day ten he started walking, peeing by himself, and even began to sing. I never thought I'd be so happy to hear a dog howl, but it was amazing!

We used to joke at university that the two outcomes for any neuro problems were death, or recovery thanks to steroid treatment, but I wasn't laughing about it this time – it was the miracle cure I had been after. I was so thankful to my lecturer, but he warned that a condition like this can come back at any time, so we decided he couldn't really go back to being a street dog, even if the hotel owners were willing to be his guardian.

Instead he moved in with Jo and became this striking-looking king of the castle at her home in Gandara. The singing dog who got his voice back. It might sound like a kids' book, and in some ways it really was a fairy tale result for Bazza.

· CHAPTER EIGHTEEN ·

THE HEARTS AND MINDS BATTLE

'Woah, woah, stop the tuk—'

Stood at the side of the road in Gandara was a kid, about eight years old, kissing a dog on his head.

Malaka and I stared as the lad confidently patted the dog, and unthinkingly gave him kisses. Malaka looked round at me and neither of us could stop grinning.

You might be wondering what the big deal was, but I can promise you it felt like one of the best moments since I'd arrived on the island. This was now more than two years since WECare had begun, and it was the first time I had seen this happen.

'In thirty-two years I have never seen a Sri Lankan kiss a dog,' Malaka announced. 'That has happened because of us, it has to be.'

It meant we were making headway in changing attitudes, slowly but surely. Our impact hadn't been instant in that respect, but the idea that dogs were worthy of this love and attention was filtering through. Things that seem like small wins can actually be really big wins, and that one kiss was a totally epic-sized win.

Pretty early on in this journey it became clear to me that there were three areas that we needed to work on in WECare, if we were to be a success – neutering and vaccination, veterinary care of individual dogs in need, and education.

By education I mean changing the local people's mindsets away from seeing dogs as vermin, to realising they are sentient beings who need love and care. I know it might sound a bit cheesy (sorry!) but I always say that WECare, but we actually want EVERYONE to care. I needed people to understand that touching a dog won't suddenly see them dying of disease; that street dogs, if in a healthy and happy state, will actually be positive rather than detrimental to the tourist industry; that they won't randomly get bitten by every passing dog.

I think education in the early days was happening almost subconsciously, in that it was happening by example, rather than specifically trying to talk to a person about issues.

I would be over the top in my contact with the animals so that people could see I wasn't afraid of them, or worried about what I might catch, so that they might believe that they shouldn't be afraid or worried either.

Set yourself up in the middle of the road, dealing hands-on with a dog who five blokes were too scared to go near five minutes ago, allow it to clamber all over you, shower it in kisses, and you are sending out a message that people take on board, whether subconsciously or consciously.

I know I go overboard with it, but I am doing it on purpose, because of the message it gives: 'I am practically snogging this dog, and I am not going to die, so why would you?'

Then I began to do impromptu stops at schools. If I was

passing a primary school, often the kids would ask me something through the fence (there are so few westerners in the area that the novelty factor still meant children regularly tried to practise their English on me). So I would respond, and then maybe go in and give a talk about what we were doing, and give them some bits to think about, like the best way to approach dogs, and how they can make a dog's life better. The kids love it, and I do too!

Later we tried to increase this side of things, by taking on an education officer who tried to get permission to go into the schools, but going through the official channels has made it tougher and it seems to be taking an age. It was much easier when a nosy child through the fence was my gateway in!

We are also looking at setting up an animal welfare course in the future at one of the universities, as nothing like that really exists at present. The more people know and care about animals the better.

The key thing for me, though, would be to go into the community centres and temples, as there is a greater sense of tradition in Sri Lanka, and the elders are the bosses of the family. Therefore it is all well and good us teaching the children something, but if they go home and Grandpa says, 'Ooh no, don't touch the dogs, they are disgusting,' then it negates everything we have said.

I have all these big plans for education, and I hope I get to put as many into play as possible, and that thinking big pays off. It's tough at times though. Any time I think people are changing, a friend will tell me they found a dog washed up on the beach with a noose around its neck, or I meet someone who tells me they purposefully aim to hit dogs in the road and have so far managed to kill four. Despite my best intentions I can't always keep my cool. I snapped at that particular guy, and called him disgusting scum.

We had a dog brought in with a fishing hook going through both sides of his mouth and into his chest, effectively attaching his jaw to his body. It was horrific. It turned out that someone had wanted a dog off their property, and had thrown the hook at him. They denied that this damage had been their intention, but I didn't believe them. The only way to get the hook through a dog's jaw like that would have been to throw it very hard, and from close range. The poor pup had then obviously shaken its head in a panic to try and dislodge the hook, only for it to then catch on its side too. He had been so worked up and running around manically that it had been hard to catch up. But eventually we were able to get hold of him and fix him up.

Another appalling injury that we have seen on dogs far too frequently is burns. People who view them as vermin will throw boiling water over them to get them to move on, which obviously leads to the most horrendous burns that, if not treated urgently, will kill the dogs.

One who sticks in my head with this was Brownie. Ah, my poor Brownie. She was brought in by her owners at about six months old with one of her sides just one huge burn wound that hadn't been dealt with instantly, and was now riddled with maggots. I have no idea why they waited so long to bring her in – sometimes people seem to think a dog will magically cure themselves – but it was horrendous and I cannot imagine the pain that pup was in. Two volunteer vets over at the time really took her on and fixed her up over the course of quite a few weeks. But then when we tried to contact her owners, they never came back. It makes you wonder. The suggestion when she'd been brought in was that someone else had thrown hot water on her, when she had wandered onto their property. But when an owner has effectively dumped their dog and has no interest in her future welfare it makes you wonder if they might have been responsible. It makes me mad and I think how I wouldn't want to send her back to someone as uncaring as them anyway. Either way it worked out well for Brownie. Her beautiful tan and white fur has grown back, and she only has a tiny scar on her side. She was rehomed to a westerner who takes her to the beach every day, and she swims and gets totally spoilt. She is loving life, which is the perfect two fingers up to whoever was responsible for those burns.

Then there is the unintentional cruelty we witness. I always aim to be patient with locals who bring their pet dogs in, as often they have very little understanding of how best to look after their pet. But sometimes it is difficult. Recently a man brought in his dog, and the general gist was she had seemed under the weather, lost her appetite, etc. But rather than give her a bit of time, or come to us with his concerns, he had asked a pharmacist for advice, who advised him to give the dog a large amount of paracetamol and caffeine to try and perk her up. It just kind of blew my mind that someone might think that was a good idea. Caffeine is never a good idea, and paracetamol is only fine in small doses, and not on the scale he had given it. I knew just how much damage was being done to the dog's insides right at that moment.

'Well done!' I snapped. 'You have probably just killed your dog.'

I know it was harsh, but I was furious at the pharmacist for dispensing the advice, mad at this man for listening to someone who knew nothing about animals, and felt utterly helpless.

True enough, she died that night, despite our attempts to save her. We never got a chance to get to the underlying problem before he dosed her up, but I am 99 per cent sure she was effectively poisoned by what her owner had fed her. A dog's body is not made in such a way that it can process human medication the way we do. That is exactly why they have a completely separate set of medications, illnesses and diseases to humans.

I'd like to think anyone reading this book would have more sense, but, if not, please don't randomly prescribe a medication for your dog, no matter what Google, a friend, or your own crazy brain might tell you. That goes for human meds, meds prescribed for another animal, or anything recommended by alternative old wives' tales! Please always seek the advice of a qualified vet.

Another owner brought in their dog Lena, as they were a bit worried that one of her eyes 'maybe had an infection'. Her eye socket was filled with maggots, and they had eaten her eye away. On what planet can you leave it like that for a few days, thinking it is 'maybe an infection'? There were maggots inside her eyeball, for god's sake!

We had to remove the remains of the eye and did a skin graft over the area and she recovered brilliantly. Then it was time for her to go back to the owner. Because yes, despite the state she had arrived in, they did actually seem to care and want Lena back.

Worryingly, she shook all the way home, and I was really concerned about placing her back with these people. I told them we would be back to check on her, and if we weren't comfortable with what we saw, she wasn't staying there. As it happens, Lena seemed really happy and settled when we popped back, and we have checked on her since and that has continued to be the case, so I can only put her shakes down to a dislike of tuk-tuks.

Generally if an owner has brought their dog into the clinic, it is a sign they care more than most. Even if it may seem neglectful by western ideas, I always want to believe the best – that it was a lack of medical understanding, a worry over payment, or a fear of blame, rather than blatant disregard for the animal's well-being.

Take the dog who was hit by a car, whose owner thought he was genuinely doing the right thing by sprinkling turmeric on the injuries, and expecting everything to heal by itself. Or the family who brought in a pup, whose foot had been hanging by a thread for five days. They were so upset, and came to visit her every day she was with us. I can't even try and fathom why they took so long to bring her to us, but it was evident they did honestly care.

I often pick up dogs out and about with wounds only to find out they are owned, and I really struggle to get my head around that. It is one thing for someone to avoid taking responsibility for a street dog, but when it is your own animal? Is that down to neglect, cruelty or a lack of education? Somewhere in the middle I think, unfortunately.

There aren't the laws to support us if we did want to remove a dog from someone, so it would effectively be theft. In these situations we can only advise and help out, and give support to help people become better informed as owners.

We sometimes see issues with dogs that have been caused by basic steps being missed by local vets, which is very frustrating. There are many who are very competent and thorough, but then there are the few others.

I had a dog brought to me a while ago who had received an amputation from a vet elsewhere on the island, but thanks to negligence of the basic sterilisation procedures, it had become infected. Other vets had then missed the infection, thinking the ulceration was caused by cancer bursting out of the skin.

It was a huge mess by the time I saw this poor dog. I had to dig out this infection that was like lumps of cottage cheese. Even though he had been amputated at the thigh, I was having to dig in right through to his pelvic bone, as the infection had spread that far and that deep. It couldn't be closed up surgically as there was nothing left to close it up with.

We were keeping the wound clean and clearing out the infection for weeks, and it would start getting better, but then worse again. We were swabbing and trying all sorts of drugs to clear it up, but the poor pup was resistant to everything. It was showing up as MRSA, and in the end we had to put him to sleep. I was furious. It literally came down to the fact that someone couldn't wash their hands before surgery. It winds me up so much that a dog lost its life because someone can't follow the most basic of hygiene rules – or then follow it up when the signs of infection appear. Because, let's face it, post-op infections are always a possible outcome, but recognise it, and do something about it.

Unfortunately, we do frequently lose dogs here from negligence. It isn't about skill, it is about effort and making sure things are done properly. All we can do is keep trying to educate on correct practice.

If I lose my temper, I cry. I cry a lot. How can I not, seeing this kind of thing day in and day out? But I cling to the understanding that these cruel people are few and far between, and they aren't necessarily fully bad, but just haven't yet made that connection with empathy yet. Let's face it, animal cruelty, and the odd person who will never have a shred of empathy, exist everywhere you go in the world. It was the large majority who could make that connection, and start treating dogs with more compassion, who I wanted to focus on.

It isn't always easy to judge whether we are winning the battle of the hearts and minds of the locals, and I think it is such a gradual change that I don't always notice it happening.

But when a tourist comments on how much healthier the dogs look in the area around Talalla Beach than the dogs they have seen everywhere else on their travels, or when a local proudly informs you that they are keeping their dog's vaccination card up to date, that you think, okay, this is working.

It is a more recent example, but a great story about educating by example comes courtesy of our manager Jo and her three dogs.

By now three of our dogs had decided that her home was also theirs. Calamity George, he of the endless treatments, was still hanging around the clinic as much as he could, and had become particularly attached to Jo. He would walk her home, and sleep in her house overnight, and bit by bit he actually moved himself in. Then when Lucy was brought in having been attacked by a wild boar, and was too flat hocked to go back home, she moved in with Jo so we could keep an eye on her. Then finally singing Barry, whose unexplained paralysis meant we wanted to keep an eye on him for life, completed the trio of dogs in her home.

They all got on well, and it was a happy little household.

The one person who wasn't so keen on the set-up was Jo's landlord, Dinush. He lived next door to her flat, and didn't like dogs one bit.

He watched the relationship between her and her three dogs at first with horror and disgust, then with amazement, then interest and, finally, understanding. Jo showed him, through all her actions, just how brilliant the dogs were, and how, when treated right, you can have such an amazing relationship with a dog. Dinush started to learn from her, and as he got used to the dogs he'd tentatively start to give them bits of food, or a little pat.

Before you knew it, the dogs were being allowed into his living room to sleep on his sofa, were being given all sorts of treats, and were even being given baths by Dinush and his children! That smart trio made sure they basically had a second home to choose from, so they could double the love. If Jo hadn't seen George, Lucy or Barry for a while, she knew exactly where she could find them.

Jo also spent time with Dinush's children, showing them how to react to dogs, how to offer them food, and what their different body language meant. Once, after Jo was bitten by a dog at a CNVR, the little girl pulled her to one side, and in a serious voice asked her, 'Jo, did you not hold your hand flat when you gave the dog a treat?'

The love-in between Dinush and the dogs became so strong that when it was his birthday, all the dogs were invited and were sat there sharing his cake – while Jo didn't get an invite and was sat at home!

That change in his mindset was incredible, and is exactly why we shouldn't be so quick to judge or assume that people aren't dog lovers. More often than not, they are just unsure. People only need to see how great a dog can be, and they start to want the same relationship with the dog. Who wouldn't?

・ CHAPTER NINETEEN ・

THE GOOD EGGS

Over time, I realised the attitude towards me and the clinic
was slowly but surely shifting. Don't get me wrong, I was
still an oddity, but I was now an accepted oddity!

I realised I was getting more smiles and calls of 'Hi, Dr Janey!'
as I walked down the street, my local shop was charging me less,
and people were finally starting to tell me about injured dogs off
their own back. It felt like I had been accepted as part of the local
community, and now rather than being suspicious or bemused by
me, they were actually looking out for me and the dogs.

There were probably a number of reasons for that:

* I had worked my arse off to try and make the
  clinic fit in with the local people, respecting
  their beliefs, even at times when I didn't agree
  with them; I'd learnt some of the language, and I
  made a real point of being direct, but polite.

- I was employing more and more local people, and I'd like to think they enjoyed their job and saw the positives of it, and would only have been helpful in passing on the message.

- The dogs on the street that these people saw every day were definitely in a much better state and hopefully they made that connection.

- I had treated many locally owned dogs at really fair (i.e. crazily cheap) prices, and been able to improve the welfare of people's pets, which was appreciated.

With this growing understanding of the clinic came more input. People were finally bringing street dogs to us that they had spotted with injuries, or giving us calls about them, without fear that they would get charged or be held accountable for any of the dog's injuries or ailments.

We've had a number of locals over time who have gone particularly above and beyond, and who Jo and I refer to as our 'good eggs'. You have those who come along quietly from time to time, hardly speaking, but clearly with empathy in their eyes. For example, there was a man from Gandara who brought in a cat who had been attacked by a lizard. We called her Lizzie (see what we did there?), fixed her up, and then the gentleman decided to adopt her – only for her to get attacked by a lizard for a second time!

A couple of months later he was back with a street pup he had come across near his home, who was in a bad way. Covered in ticks and fleas, there were maggots burrowed into his head and neck, creating a real network under his skin. The poor mite had to be sedated and have them removed, as well as being treated for tick fever, but he was young enough that he bounced back, and the kind local then took him in too.

There was no drama or need for recognition, just a kind man, doing what he could for the animals in need he came across.

There is a group of ex-pats who are generally pretty good at spotting when a street dog is genuinely in need and bringing them in where possible, or letting us know their whereabouts. They also realise that we are a charity and often will very kindly contribute towards the costs of fixing any animal they alert us to.

Then there are the crucial guardians, some of whom are really active, such as Surangi, a lovely local lady who, along with her British husband, keeps an eye on quite a few dogs, and is always rescuing others. She looks out for any problems on Facebook and will go round and find dogs to bring to us, or pay for them to be helped. She has a heart of gold, and hardly a week goes by when we don't hear from her about some animal or other in distress.

She brought in a grey dog once called Angel, who came from a village a couple of hours away. This poor dog had a halo tumour that effectively made her look like she was balancing a pizza on the top of her head – see where she got her name from?

It turns out that Angel had been living with it for years, but after treatment we were able to send her home looking as good as new.

What was lovely to hear was that a villager asked this woman: 'Do you have a magic wand? How are you getting these dogs fixed?' And she was able to tell them about WECare, and our work, and explained that we were the magic wand!

Mali's guardian continued to look out for him and keep him well fed with all her scraps, but I was getting worried that he was losing his eyesight quite quickly. Some of the younger bolder dogs were getting cheeky, and encroaching into his territory, bumping him along up the road a bit, and with his eyes not being as good, living so close to the road wasn't great.

I stopped one day to give him a quick cuddle and a man came out of his house and said, 'This dog is disgusting, he shouldn't be around here.'

It didn't sit well with me, and I was uncomfortable for the rest of the day worrying that this guy might actually do something to harm Mali, or force him to move on. Although he is a tough and clever dog, there was no getting past his age – fifteen by then. He is a real anomaly in age terms. A street dog is doing well if he has lived to six or eight years out here, so Mali really is positively ancient!

There was nothing for it, I decided, but to move him in with me. I got Emily to pick him up later that day, and that was that, he became dog number five living with me, alongside Benji, Tilly, Stitch and Lottie.

Mali fought a lot with Benji in the beginning, as they battled to work out who was going to be top dog, both of the house, and in ownership of me. It was less about physical fights, but more a battle of the pee …

Mali was a total menace in his need to piss everywhere to try and mark his new territory. It didn't matter to him if he was in the house or out. I'd get in and set my rucksack down, and two seconds later look up to see Mali pissing on it, like, 'Yup, she's my mum'.

'Mali! Go on, get off!' I'd yell in frustration, but as he walked away Benji would be hot on his heels, pissing on my bag too, in a need to get the final word: 'Nope, she's my mum!'

It was a real stinky battle, but luckily things soon settled down. The younger dogs don't let Mali sleep on the veranda in the day with them, but he is quite happy off to the side with Lottie and they look really cute just chilling on their bed together. They have become good pals.

None of the dogs sleep outside at night though. They would be fine with the temperatures, of course, but I worry about snakes so it doesn't seem worth the risk. They have their own room in the house with bean bags that they all sleep on, although Mali will always try his luck and head for the sofa. He is still a big puppy at heart really. He isn't allowed on it, but will have a paddy if you try and move him off it onto the floor. No ground for him when a softer option is available. So much for being a tough street dog!

Soft bed aside, he still has the street dog need not to feel trapped, but to have the freedom to roam. So within a week, he had chewed a hole in the back fence to create an exit. Once it was there he would use it each morning to go out for a quick sniff and the toilet, then after he had done that he would come back inside and sleep all day. He is really happy in his 'retirement', but the need to know he has his freedom, even if he doesn't use it, is strong in him.

Within two weeks he had also sussed out how to open the doors, whereas the other guys took for ever to work that out.

The other dogs follow him out sometimes and go off on their adventures, which always worries me, but I like it too, as they love it so much. Mind you, they are having a turf war with some of the neighbourhood dogs at the moment, so it's not always easy for them to get past the front gate. At times, if I want to get them to Talalla Beach for a good run along there on a day off, I have to get Chaminda to come and load all the guys in the tuk-tuk, just to get them past the dogs they are arguing with and to the beach. You can't say they aren't spoilt – they have their own personal chauffeur to drive them a few hundred metres for a day at the seaside!

The best of the WECare good eggs for me was always Malaka, but unfortunately our working relationship was about to come to an end. An incident happened at the clinic involving Malaka and another staff member, and when I confronted him about it he denied all knowledge. I had absolute, total belief in the guy, so took his word for it, and said to everyone else, 'I don't know what happened, but Malaka is innocent, he wouldn't lie to me.'

But it turns out he had. Malaka, who I thought of as a brother, and trusted with everything, had broken that trust. I had to confront him again on Boxing Day 2017 with irrefutable proof, and this time he tried to confess and explain, but by then it was too late. We had to let him go. It was such a shock to the system that someone I believed to be so good to the core had behaved in a way that left me feeling so badly let down. It broke my heart really. I also worried it would have a negative impact on the dogs as he had been so key to WECare, and I didn't know how I would cope without him. I thought he was indispensable, but I also knew that if I was to run this as a proper, respectable charity, it was the only action we could take.

Malaka now lives back with his family in the centre of the island and, despite everything, I still love him to bits and consider him a true friend. We went through far too much together, and he had my back in the early days when no one else did, and I will never forget that. We are still in touch, and maybe he will be able to work at WECare again one day, but I don't know if it would be the same.

No one was going to be able to replace Malaka, but dependable Vinura started to take on a bigger role and become my main go-to guy. It had been the running joke that I shouted for Malaka every time I needed help with something, but now yells of 'Vinura!' could be heard echoing around the clinic.

Every time he would come running into the room, with these massive flip-flops that were far too big for him, and jump to attention in front of me with a grin. It was a smile that meant you could never be mad at him – not that he ever got things wrong anyway. His enthusiasm and desire to be involved was quite special, and there wasn't anything he wouldn't do for the dogs, or WECare as a whole.

It sounds strange to say that a seventeen-year-old volunteer could inspire me, but he did. Everything for him was just so purely and simply about the dogs, that if I was getting sidetracked by politics or the annoying intricacies of running a charity, his refreshing and clear attitude could pull me back. He was living proof that wisdom often has nothing to do with age.

Often when people think of WECare they think it is just me. But these good eggs, and so many more that have helped over the years, show just how much caring for these dogs is a team effort. I also think that most people are good eggs deep down, they just sometimes need it drawn out of them a bit.

CHAPTER TWENTY

THE TRIPOD CLAN

I know I said that the wise old dogs like Mali and Eddie are my favourites, but I also do have a real soft spot for the 'tripods' who pass through the clinic. That resilience and adaptability to bounce back after losing a limb, and tackle life with the same gusto as before, is bloody inspirational.

They also show what can be done with a bit of time and patience from our end, as removing a limb and getting a dog back and walking can be quite a complicated and long business.

Sadly not everyone agrees with me that these tripods are great though, and some people see them as incomplete, or damaged dogs. Remember the family who stopped me putting Belle to sleep, but then wouldn't take her once she had three legs? They are not alone. Whereas elsewhere they might be seen as quite endearing, getting a three-legged dog rehomed here is practically impossible as people think they are going to be much harder work.

By now, original tripod Belle had decided she had had enough of the clinic (yeah, I love you too, Belle!), and decided to return to her nomadic life. She still keeps local, and is regularly spotted at the end of our road in the morning, waiting for the fish seller to pass on his rounds, in case she gets lucky. A neighbour a few doors down from the clinic also has a bed that Belle uses when she is feeling like it. I am sad not to see her as much, but everyone knows to report sightings to me when they spot her, and ultimately it makes me happy. My strong, gorgeous Belle is living exactly the kind of life I would only ever have thought was a fantasy for that damaged little pup, and I still smile when I think of all we managed to get through together.

Polly, the first patient in our actual clinic who had a leg removed, is still doing well too, although her street dog instincts have definitely kicked back in. After enjoying being a bit more of a settled, fussed-over dog, first in the clinic, and then with Malaka's friend, she moved herself out and down the road to a hotel for a bit, and then set up home in the petrol station. Yup, there is no accounting for these dogs' tastes! But the guys there are happy to have her, and feed her each day, and she likes the freedom of sleeping outside, and roaming off on her adventures. To see her happy and living life with all the confidence of a four-legged dog is just perfect.

There have been some other incredible three-legged little warriors who have particularly stood out for me.

In June 2018, I'd been working late and was driving home with Emily, when we went past a coconut husk in the road. My brain processed what I had seen as we carried on, and something didn't sit right, so we turned around and went back to check. It was lucky I listened to those nagging doubts, because it was actually a little black, tan and white puppy. Scooping up newly named Lucky, we got her back to the clinic to discover she had mange and a fractured femur, most likely caused by a run in with a vehicle.

The next day we went back to check the area, as a puppy that young is unlikely to be on her own. Sure enough, we ended up finding her sister, Sunny, bizarrely with an almost identical injury.

As it happens, two other puppies came in at the same time with broken limbs, and we had all four of them bandaged up in bright colours, hobbling around the place, tumbling over each other, and shamelessly looking for attention.

After a while, Sunny and the other two puppies recovered, and were ready for rehoming, but things weren't as striaightforward for Lucky. Her break was up close to the hip, and when we took the cast off it was clear it hadn't healed the way we had hoped, so amputation was the only option. It turned out there were several fragments to her break, so it was more complicated than I had realised, and even the amputation was a tricky process.

This meant Lucky's recovery took slightly longer than usual, but she soon pulled through, and moved into the garden with the other dogs, while she got used to her new tripod set-up.

These are the kinds of situations where I used to get very frustrated that we didn't have an X-ray machine. I could only make decisions on the kind of fracture a dog had by feel and the way a dog responds, so it is never an exact science. Having an image to work from lets you know the situation before the surgery. It might be a simple fracture, i.e. one fracture, or a comminuted fracture which means there are bits everywhere. Each type needs different equipment: generally a plate for a simple fracture, and wires and pins for a comminuted one. Then different drill bits are needed, and it can be quite stressful going into the operation as a surgeon without that prior knowledge and preparation.

Post-op images let you know that a break is healing in the right way. You need to get the gap between the two bone parts to a maximum of three millimetres, or it is never going to heal, so those X-rays let you know if there has been a non-union, and you are going to have to go back in.

If I knew with imaging that surgery had worked, a dog could be in and out in three to four weeks with a perfect repair. But without a picture we had to put the leg in a splint for six to eight weeks, changing and checking by feel each week, without the same guarantee that the bones would have fused as well.

I was desperate for an X-ray machine and an ultrasound, but to buy both and kit out the room was going to cost £30,000 – money that we just didn't have. So for the time being, I just had to do my best by dogs like Lucky.

Then in September 2018, our clinic manager Jo was in Dikwella bus station when she came across a young cream-coloured puppy who was missing part of her right back leg. She was hobbling around with part of the bone completely exposed. It looked totally raw and incredibly painful. It wasn't clear what had caused it – probably an RTA – but Bonnie, as we decided to call her, was sweet-natured, if a little unsure. Incredibly the locals told us she had been in this state for about ten days before Jo happened to stumble across her. Once again, I've got to ask how the hell no one thought to actually do anything about it. By this stage I felt we were well known in the area, and that all people had to do was make one call to us. They didn't even have to bring the dog in if that wasn't an option for them, nor were they required to pay for the treatment. One phone call, to end that suffering.

But Bonnie had kept going, doing incredibly well to survive that long without pain relief or help.

Her swollen belly told us that she was probably suffering from worms; she was crawling with fleas and her blood count was really low. A low blood count – i.e. a low percentage of red blood cells in the body – is common in unhealthy dogs, but as they carry oxygen through the body, it is important to get that sorted.

There was no option to do anything with her leg except

amputate it, and help her adjust to life on three.

The wound stayed swollen for a few days, but soon started to settle, and physio began.

Luckily she took to her three legs really quickly and was soon out in the garden with the other dogs, including fellow tripod Lucky.

The two of them spent their days lazing around in the sun, barking at the trees if they spotted any monkeys, and keeping in line any other youngsters who ended up outside with them. They liked play fighting together, half-heartedly mouthing at each other, before collapsing into a heap for a snooze in the afternoon sun. Instant best friends, who were perfectly matched.

We couldn't put either Lucky or Bonnie back on the street, as while we have no issue putting a three-legged adult dog back out there if we think they have the hardiness and experience to pick up life where they left off, it wouldn't be the case with a puppy. They would have no chance.

People assume three-legged dogs will come with a bunch of problems. Even people with the best of intentions, who say they are keen to help out with a tripod, come and visit, then spot a four-legged pup and veer off over to them.

It is occasionally possible when the dogs are still puppies for them to be rehomed, as you do get the odd kind-hearted soul. We had one dog in called Little John who came in needing an amputation, and his potential adoptees were worried about his ability to get around, so Jo put him on the floor and he charged around everywhere as though to prove them wrong. It worked, and they were like, 'Great, we will take him!' So that was a lovely ending. But unfortunately as the dogs get older, it pretty much becomes a lost cause.

Both Bonnie and Lucky were lined up for separate adoptions, but they fell through last minute, and as they had both grown into teenage dogs by then, the chances were getting slimmer. So despite the fact both were such gorgeous-looking dogs with the loveliest personalities, there were no takers and they became some of WECare's long-term residents.

Getting a three-legged dog to walk isn't always easy and can be a long process. Once the stump is healing, physio begins, as they now have to find a different way of walking. Muscles might have become weak as they recovered, and certain muscles now need to be stronger and used in a slightly different way to before, to get around.

There is no getting around the fact that learning to walk on three legs isn't a dignified process. It can only happen from actually standing and practising, and it is all about trial and error. So yes, the poor doggos will look like Bambi on ice, probably fall on their face, and will let you know with every angry glare that they hold you fully responsible for this indignity. But if you are to encourage them to be independent again, it is a necessary evil.

Then suddenly one day it will click and you see them bouncing around, as though they never had anything but three legs. It is incredible and cheers up any miserable day. The wounds heal quickly and, before you know it, they are holding their own with the other dogs as though that fourth leg was never needed in the first place.

Physio is an important job with many four-legged dogs too. Sadly, we get a lot of RTA cases where the dogs still have their legs intact, but they are suffering with paralysis, mainly to their hind legs.

Treatment might begin with the dog having their legs rubbed

to get blood flowing, stretched in and out and rotated, or the toe pinched to encourage them to do the movement themselves.

As they start to get more movement in their limbs, we will get them into the water for some physio there. There is nothing cuter than seeing the dogs bobbing around in the sea in their little life jackets, starting to get their legs back in action.

Back in the clinic, the tripods were long-term residents, along with Eddie, Tootsy Bear and a couple of brothers called Dot and Seal.

Those two came to us via a CNVR in Dikwella in October 2016. They were puppies at the time and both feeble, hairless little things, thanks to a bad case of mange. Back at the hospital they were given the usual treatment – Advocate – and it worked its magic on Seal, but for some reason it didn't work on Dot. There was no way Seal was going up for adoption without Dot though. We had already realised these are two proper little peas in a pod, who can't function without each other, so we kept them both in for longer.

A new medicine called Bravecto had just been released in the UK, so we tried that on Dot instead, and finally his fur started growing back, albeit quite coarsely. He had such pale skin but loved chilling in the sunshine, so in the meantime we had to constantly keep him coated in suncream! He made out that it was a big chore and he was doing us a favour, but Dot definitely secretly liked the attention that came with his suncream sessions.

Finally they were ready to be rehomed, but unfortunately their recovery had taken a while, and they were no longer these cute little pups. Just like everywhere else in the world, adoption is so much easier if you are a cute little pup, rather than a gangly teenager.

Dot and Seal seem like a bit of a handful on first impression and can be quite barky towards strangers, but once they have you sussed and decide you are all right (assuming you are), they are absolute legends. It makes me sad for them, that they don't have a new home. Not that there won't always be a home for them at WECare, but here they always have to put up with a constant stream of other dogs passing through. They have seen everyone come and go, and are losing their patience with the endless stream of new puppies trying to hang off their ears. They just want to relax in the garden, and have started to develop short tempers with the pups, which isn't great for anyone. We try and get them out as much as possible, and they love joining the vollies on walks into the village. Seeing them trot around side by side, changing direction in sync, and with the same ear flopped forward while the other is up, the brotherly love is stronger than I've ever seen in other dogs. Dot got a wound on his bum at one point and had a brief stay indoors at the clinic, and Seal was absolutely lost without him. My heart breaks for the pair of them really.

I'd have them back at my house if I didn't have so many animals already. I have to remind myself sometimes that the reason we got a clinic and dog accommodation space was so that my house wasn't overflowing with dogs!

• CHAPTER TWENTY-ONE •

SUMMER OF HELL

I'm such a dog person that cats have to work hard to really sneak into my affections. But three of them in particular have got under my skin. One of them, Delilah, was found as a tiny kitten near the clinic by a vollie, and despite her size was so confident and feisty from day one that I decided to adopt her. She's with me as I write this.

Another kitten crossed my path during a CNVR programme in Arugam Bay on the east coast. We came across this little ginger mite hiding under a boat with a huge wound on his side and a broken back leg. I fell in love with Pumpkin instantly, figured his injuries were easily fixable, and decided to adopt him. I bandaged him up, and he made himself at home at the CNVR site in the day, playing with one of the puppies, and at night he would snuggle into my neck as I slept.

Three nights later Pumpkin started to breathe through his mouth, which in cats is not a good sign. His chest sounded clear, but without the help of diagnostic imaging, I wasn't sure what was going on, so I decided to take him down to our makeshift clinic and tap his chest, i.e. remove any liquid or gas from between his lungs and chest wall. It turned out there were twelve millilitres of blood in there, and as we were draining it he stopped breathing.

I desperately tried CPR, but with no luck, then cried my eyes out, and beat myself up for not having noticed sooner. Little Pumpkin's life felt like it had been cut off far too soon.

I wasn't doing well with cats. Before that cutie, in spring 2018 I adopted a tiny kitten called Milo. He was a shy little thing and living in my house while he built up his strength and confidence. But one day my friend came through the front door and Benji pushed past her, and ran over to the kitten, desperate to play with him. Before we could stop Benji, he picked Milo up and shook him, but it was too rough, and broke his neck and killed him. Benji instantly dropped Milo, and seemed shocked at what had happened. I was horrified and felt so guilty. When Benji saw me sobbing, he lay unmoving by Milo's grave for the whole day afterwards.

I was devastated that such a tiny new life had been taken, and in my home, where animals should be safe, but two days later things were to get much worse.

We were just approaching Vinura's 18th birthday, and wondering what we could do to mark the occasion for him, when on 5 May 2018 we got the devastating call. A bus on the wrong side of the road had knocked Vinura off his motorbike, and he had been killed.

We all went into shock. This guy was a part of everything at the clinic, and people were breaking down crying in disbelief that this could happen to such a good kid, just starting out in life.

I know people seem to always say 'Oh he was amazing' when someone dies, but he really was. An amazing soul who didn't have a bad bone in his body; a total sweetheart, and someone who had made a real impact in his short time at WECare.

Vinura lit up every room he walked into. You could be in the worst mood, then see his face and be instantly cheered up, as he was so bright and breezy, a real bundle of energy.

The funeral arrangements tend to start almost straight away in Sri Lanka and then go on for seven days. For the first two or three days Vinura's body was laid out, and family and friends were invited to go and sit with him. There were different rituals, chants and prayers. There were also alms, where you are asked to donate items to the temple, such as sugar. We wanted to give to Vinura's family directly as we knew they were struggling to cover funeral costs and he had done so much for us, but it had to go to the temple as that was custom.

At the actual ceremony, I was at the back in tears, when I was unexpectedly called up to the front. 'Dr Janey, could you come and say a few words?'

My Sinhala is not good enough to say everything I wanted to, so I spoke in English about how Vinura will always feel like an integral part of WECare, and hoped that the congregation understood. I said we were all privileged to know him, and how I would never forget him.

In the days, weeks and months afterwards, the clinic felt weird and empty. I don't think any of us had really accepted Vinura's death – and maybe still haven't. It is like he has gone on a long holiday and will pop back up, running round the garden, playing with the dogs and not caring if he gets filthy, while they all bundle on top of him.

But Vinura would want us to push on, and would have been devastated if the dogs were to suffer at all, so we tried our best. The reality, though, is that DN lost a part of him that day – we all did.

I'd always known the roads were bad – people pulling up to junctions, looking, seeing a car coming, and pulling out anyway; women riding pillion on scooters, juggling toddlers and babies without safety equipment; trucks with makeshift sofas in the back, and families tightly packed onto them. Accidents waiting to happen, with potentially deadly consequences. Scooters might be the easiest method for getting around, but they also leave you very vulnerable, and that same year I kept seeing the impact it can have first hand.

Luckily I have never yet had an accident (touch wood) but Jo was the next to fall victim to the roads. An underage drunk driver pulled out in front of her, and she had no time and no place to swerve to, so went into him. She was angry and shaken up, and had to fork out on bike repairs, but ultimately we were all thankful that her injuries were superficial.

I lost two other friends to the roads that year – another on a motorbike, and one who was killed along with their driver, when a bus hit their taxi. Looking at the figures, seven people are killed on the roads every day. A heartbreaking stat for such as small country.

We pushed on in the clinic, but it was doubly hard as there had been difficulties with the visas for a set of new staff who had been due to join us in the spring and still weren't here. It meant we were working to our limit, and everyone was tired and stressed, and I knew my patience was wearing a bit thin.

Then a really young puppy called Buzz, who was only about four or five weeks old, was brought in with a snare on his leg. It was no doubt a snare left out for wild pigs that Buzz had been unfortunate enough to wander into instead. The leg had died off by the time he made it to us, so there was no other option than to amputate his leg. He was so small that using the injectable anaesthetic that we use for adult dogs would have been dangerous, so we chose to operate under gas anaesthesia, which is much safer to use when they are as tiny as Buzz.

Only a handful of vets have access to it in Sri Lanka, and none that I am aware of outside of Colombo and the vet school in Kandy. But you always use gas in the UK, so when I'd first arrived, I'd found it hard operating without it as, while injectables are much easier, they come with a much higher risk.

The problem is that injectable anaesthesia is like taking a pill – once it is inside a patient, you have no control over the dose, or any reaction they might have. Gas, though, is more like an adjustable tap that you can turn up or down, or taper as needed, appropriate to the patient.

Gas goes to the lungs and then directly to where it is needed, then it stops working when it is turned off. Injectables are stored in the fat and muscle and released over time, so the effects can be felt for a long time afterwards.

Unfortunately, gas is much more expensive, and the skill level to administer it is so much higher. It takes a lot of specialised study before you are even allowed to touch a patient, so when I first arrived and was working on my own, or with assistants who weren't qualified nurses, it wasn't an option.

By this stage, though, we were super lucky that we were able to afford it, and that I had a nurse out here to operate the gas for me. Buzz's operation was a success, and three weeks later he was through his isolation period, and his leg 'stump' had healed up well enough for him to join the others in the garden. He was so small and had such a big puppy belly that at first he couldn't work out how to get around on three legs, but after stumbling around in circles for a while, he eventually sussed it out. It was super cute to watch him tumbling around the garden, and we made a video of him, thinking this was going to be one of our happy endings.

Then one evening at about five o'clock, he did a tiny vomit. Being sick is common in dogs, and pups in particular frequently get gastrointestinal upsets, but we brought him in overnight to be sure. The next day when I got in, I was gutted to find his poor lifeless body. I instantly started berrating myself, wondering what I had missed. I carried out a post-mortem, which isn't pleasant at the best of times, and even less so when you have built up a relationship with the dog, but I couldn't find anything. The most likely diagnoses I could come up with was distemper or another infectious cause of gastroenteritis, although I felt I was reaching out in a bid to have some kind of conclusion. Distemper didn't really make sense as he had been vaccinated, and there had been so little sign of anything before he had died.

But then suddenly another puppy got sick and died, and then another. Five of the puppies were from the same litter, and we had brought them back from a CNVR day on the east coast. As always, these dogs had been through the obligatory isolation period when they arrived, so if they had brought something in with them, they had incubated it throughout that period.

Two others that had come in separately also went the same way. All the pups showed very little sign of being ill, but would vomit, then pass away within hours. Suddenly we had lost eight puppies in the space of a week. It was devastating and I spent ages researching for any possible cause.

We isolated the dogs individually as much as possible and were hotter than ever on hygiene standards. It was awful, coming in to bad news, day after day, and with tiny pups that should just be starting out on their lives.

I messaged my crew of experts back in the UK, but no one was able to come up with any more suggestions. I am aware that there may still be diseases that are new to me, or specific to Sri Lanka that I have not yet come across, so I needed to understand. How could so many young dogs die in my care without explanation?

I never did get to the bottom of it, and the only saving grace was that it seemed to end as quickly as it had arrived.

I didn't have long to think, as my poor boy, Ticky, was hit by the cursed summer. Ticky, one of our first residents at the clinic, who had been found with paralysed back legs at the end of our road, had been living a happy life with us for the two and a half years since.

Soon after everything had happened with the pups, Ticky started to go off his food, and wasn't seeming himself. Then one day in June we came in to find him collapsed on the floor, his legs having given way again. I started working through all the options to see what his symptoms were and work out a possible cause. He could hardly open his eyes and it quickly became clear he had become photophobic – really sensitive to light. Everything was pointing towards it being a neurological problem, but I had no idea what could have set it off. He was fully vaccinated and had been for years, so whatever the pups had – if it was distemper – shouldn't have impacted on him.

I thought back to his original paralysis and wondered if that had been down to a neurological cause as opposed to an RTA, as, after all, we hadn't witnessed what had happened.

You always assume paralysis is caused by damage to the spinal cord, usually from fractures or compressive injuries, but you never know. Maybe he had a central lesion, such as a brain tumour, or a spinal tumour that was getting bigger and starting to press on the wrong bits. But then, again, it didn't seem likely that this would have taken two years to reappear, and I was sure something like that would have progressed more quickly. Or maybe he had caught a mild version of whatever the pups had and, if so, his neurological system was shot, his neurons weren't handling it. The reality was it could have been many things, either linked to the pups, or happening as just a horrible coincidence.

Back in the UK I would have sent Ticky for an MRI (magnetic resonance imaging) that can give you a detailed image of the inside of the body, but of course I didn't have the equipment for that. In the meantime he had no control over his bowels or bladder, and his eyes were very sensitive to the light. It was bizarre, and awful to watch.

I tried steroids, and he certainly improved. He went from struggling to eat to being ravenous and able to open his eyes. I kept him in the office with me every day, looking after him, feeding him, and just showing him love.

Unfortunately, his improvement didn't go beyond that and he still couldn't walk, or even really stand. I kept focusing on all the other dogs who had pulled through when you thought they were right on the brink. Looking back, it was clear no one wanted to broach the idea with me of putting him to sleep, because he was my boy, and I didn't want to give up on him.

After six weeks I realised that despite my best efforts, he was just existing, not living. I would walk in to find he had peed and was just lying in it as he couldn't do anything else and, despite his improved appetite, he looked like he was wasting away. I had to face up to the fact that I was keeping him alive for my sake, and the kindest thing for him was to let him go.

There is nothing worse than putting your own dog to sleep (or a dog that you are so close to he feels like he is yours).

We always PTS (put to sleep) by injection, and I decided to do it in the garden for two reasons. For Ticky, so that he didn't feel stressed, and was in his happy place, but also so that the other dogs could know he was gone. He quietly slipped away, and his best friend Tootsy wouldn't leave his side, and then took to wandering listlessly around the garden, not looking at me, as though I was responsible. After a few days she went the other way and attached herself to me, wanting cuddles all the time. There is never any question for me that dogs grieve for each other, and go through a process much the way humans do.

When dogs die at the clinic, I get the boys to bury them around the perimeter of the gardens. But this time I asked them to put Ticky in the ground right outside the office. That way he would always be close to us as we worked.

The dynamics in the garden changed overall with Ticky's departure. Despite being a castrated male and a tripod, it was clear he had been the boss, and now with no one in charge out there, things fell apart a bit. Dot and Seal started relentlessly bullying the others, to the point where they had to be moved to their own separate enclosure. It didn't feel as cohesive between the garden dogs.

I miss Ticky a lot. He was just so lovely. It was such a weird and sad way to lose him and, with everything else, I wasn't sure I could stand it. I know you often get a run of bad luck, but this just felt like too much to cope with, one thing after another. In a way I struggle to think back over that whole summer, as though my mind has actually tried to block it out. I think self-preservation means the fewer memories I have from then, the better. It was such a shitty time, I began to think I couldn't cope, and the threads that were holding me together were starting to unravel.

CHAPTER TWENTY-TWO

BURNOUT

The new staff finally arrived, and I decided that was it, I was going to give myself some time off. I'd spent the last few years working with minimal (aka no) breaks, and deep down I knew I was hitting a bit of a mental brick wall, so it felt like I needed a time out. Besides, I was turning thirty, so this was a biggy. Time to celebrate!

I treated myself to a surf trip to the Maldives, then returned to Sri Lanka and my family and friends came out to visit for a big party, organised by some of my lovely staff. It was a perfect few weeks, exactly what I needed.

But then when everyone left and I was due to get stuck back into work, I couldn't. With the distraction of my birthday over, I fell apart. It wasn't just a case of, 'Oh, back to reality with a bump, don't love this', I literally couldn't function to get myself out of bed and into the clinic. While I wanted to get back to WECare, my brain and my body had other ideas. I was tearful, anxious, tired, and my mind was constantly running through everything that I believed I was doing wrong. It was clear I was suffering from some kind of burnout.

I was shocked, as I always think of myself as a bit of a tough cookie, not the kind of person who falls apart. But I guess that is what most people think – until it happens to them. I thought I was managing and that I was all right, but clearly I wasn't.

I tried to assess what was happening, and realised I had worked non-stop since arriving in the country, often sixteen-hour days, dealing with the most heartbreaking cases and difficult decisions. I was so immersed in it that my job had become my everything, and I didn't feel like I needed anything else in my life.

If I wasn't being hands-on with the dogs, I was working on fundraising or dealing with emails, or social media. And if I wasn't working in Sri Lanka, I was working in Dubai or the UK. I'd basically done a bit of a Maggie Thatcher and slept four hours a night for four years.

I felt like I couldn't slow down – these dogs needed me. If I wasn't there looking after them and helping them every hour of the day, I was as good as condemning some of them to death, and I couldn't let that happen.

But no matter how hard I worked, my to-do list just seemed to grow longer, and the tasks got bigger. If there was one emotion I had felt more than any in those first four years, it was overwhelmed.

Put like that, I guess it was inevitable that something was eventually going to have to give.

I took six weeks off to try and get myself together. Jo was an absolute godsend. She basically held the clinic together and made sure everything kept running smoothly. The arrival of the new staff meant for once it wasn't an understaffed clinic, but the odd time I popped in I felt even more guilty. I knew these new arrivees had come with an expectation of working with me, especially after the BBC documentary, but any time they saw me I was an exhausted, teary mess. Knowing I was failing to live up to the picture of the me they must have had before arriving felt like horrible extra pressure.

At first I spent the time in bed, then dragged myself to a lounger at the beach, but I repeatedly disappeared down a bit of a mental wormhole. I kept wondering what I was doing here. No matter how many hours I put in, I couldn't get on top of things, and there were so many thousands of dogs in need. I could see all the possibilities, so I'd been working myself into the ground to make it happen. I'd been push, push, pushing myself, and made everything full-on, as I wanted the best outcomes.

But now it felt like I couldn't see the woods for the trees. The highs and the lows were getting too much, I was craving some days where things were just normal and ordinary.

On a personal level, I realised I had neglected everything else in my life but the dogs. I worried that I'd been a crap girlfriend, an unreliable friend, and a useless daughter.

I'd had a couple of relationships while in Sri Lanka, but they were impossible to sustain. What kind of guy is going to put up with my lifestyle, and what kind of girlfriend can I honestly be to them? They have to deal with me going through all sorts of emotions, working all hours, cancelling for emergencies, and basically knowing that they come second behind the dogs.

It is the same with friends. They all know that dogs come first, but if I'm honest, I was lonely. I struggle sometimes when talking to the other ex-pats out here, as lots of them have moved to the tourist spots and are running guesthouses and hanging out all day with people who are here on holiday. In the meantime, I am seeing the Sri Lanka behind the Instagram filter, which includes some pretty grim stuff. In a way, I think what I've seen gives me more of a real love for the country, but it means we aren't having the same experiences, and don't always understand each other. At times we can be on different levels of understanding, which can make the friendships feel superficial at times.

It means my circle of true friends is very small, but luckily when I was having a real meltdown, a few of them were truly there for me. People who would just come and sit in the house, and eat ice cream with me and listen, who proved that when push came to shove, they had my back.

As for how I treated myself, spending time on me pretty much didn't exist. I realised I never took any time for myself. Even getting a moment to wash my hair sometimes felt like a big ask. I had dreams of surfing every week, travelling, and meeting new people, but it wasn't happening. Even most of my social occasions were built around the clinic – a fundraising event, or a meeting in a bar with someone who might be able to help us out in some way.

Because I was going through burnout, I was only focusing on the negatives, so over those six weeks I started to remind myself of all the positives of my Sri Lankan life, as well as coming up with ways to help change the parts that had become too much. And overriding everything was, of course, the knowledge that none of it was enough of a reason to abandon all the street dogs that still needed my help. They come first.

I started to try and set boundaries, to say no, and to give myself a bit of space to breathe from time to time. Getting a work-life balance just isn't something that comes naturally, so I started to work at it. It's not easy though.

I tried to take some time off recently. I booked a hotel down the coast, with the idea of going to a party, and then surfing the next day. But I'd only just checked into the hotel when I got a message asking me to go back. A dog had come in with his eye hanging out thanks to a trauma to his head, and the volunteer vet didn't feel confident dealing with it.

I was an hour away and was just about to finally relax for twenty-four hours. My initial reaction was to jump in a tuk-tuk, as the dog's well-being will always come first. But then I realised that even were I back at the clinic, my first action wouldn't be to operate at this time of night, but would be to give pain relief, and see if that worked. There was no saving the eye, and it had been out for a few days already, so I would be looking to let the dog settle in until the next day.

I asked the vollie to try and eliminate the pain, on the understanding that if it didn't work, I'd come back and operate straight away. She was able to do this easily, but I still felt so much guilt. I tried my best to enjoy the evening but instead I ended up in tears. There were dogs out there suffering, what was I doing, trying to have fun?

The rational bit of my mind knows I need time off. I try and tell myself I will do a better job if I have had a break, that I will be more alert and focused. But any time I try and spend time away from the clinic, something happens with a dog, and before I know it, I am back in. I worry I am being too controlling, but we have a duty to the dogs to do everything in the best way possible, and I don't feel that because these are street dogs, they should have any lesser a standard of care. When volunteer vets come out to help, it is a real relief, but they come with varying skill sets and at different levels of their career. It can be a real shock for them to be thrown into WECare life, and it is not fair to expect them to deal with something they have never come across before – either for their sake or the animals'. It means that even with their help, I can rarely step completely away from the clinic.

This applies to times when I am not trying to take a break, but need to do work elsewhere. So, for example, I know that if the charity is to survive and have a future, I need to secure better funding, but doing that takes time, and might involve sitting at home writing an application for a charity grant. Inevitably enough though, part way through that I will get a call to go in, and what else can I do?

I began paying myself a salary for the first time since being here. Nothing groundbreaking, but enough to make sure I could at least cover my rent and living expenses without having to do locum stints in Dubai, or max out even more credit cards!

We also introduced charges for owned dogs at the clinic. As word had spread that we treated all dogs for free, the number of people bringing their own pets to us was shooting up. I have always said we won't turn away any dog in need, but it felt like we were getting drawn into treating dogs with small problems, and losing sight of our main objective – the street dogs – and needed to pull that back in.

We didn't ask for anything extravagant, as I didn't want people to be put off, but as an idea, here are a few prices off our list:

- Rabies vaccine: 300 rupees (£1.50)
  Typical UK price: £32.60.
- Male neutering: 2,000 rupees (£10)
  Typical UK price: £200.

- Hospital stay: 600–1,000 rupees (£2.50–£5) per day, depending on whether a mild case or in need of isolation. Typical UK price: £45.

People think our costs must be much cheaper than the UK, but as so much of our equipment and treatments come from there – drapes, swabs, spay kits etc. – it isn't massively lower. Unfortunately our costs always outway what we charge the owners and we heavily subsidise it, but we can't increase it, or we risk people not actually following through with the treatment.

We also decided to extend our fundraising, with one of the new staff helping out. I run a ball each autumn in Newcastle, which is well supported and brings in a large amount of much needed funds. But we wanted to push more in other areas – sponsored dog walks, quizzes, challenges, online adoptions for the dogs, etc.

All these changes helped with getting the WECare buzz going again for me, and I was really relieved when I felt up to getting stuck back in. Plus Jo had pulled together all the figures on the dogs we had treated by November 2018, and looking at those made me realise that despite the financial, emotional, physical and mental hardships, it really had all been worth it.

WECare had treated 4,098 dogs, neutered 4,495, and vaccinated 6,898. It was amazing to see the figures, and felt like such an achievement. It meant we had literally changed the lives of thousands of dogs, not to mention the knock-on effect it would have for thousands more. If I was to pull off the long-term plans that were forming in my head, those numbers were soon going to be shooting up too. I needed to push on in the clinic, and keep it growing and developing. There was no going back from this – onwards and upwards!

• CHAPTER TWENTY-THREE •

ADOPTION AND RECONNECTING

Sometimes I miss the magic of the early days, when it was just me, Chaz and Malaka doing our thing, out in the tuk-tuk, operating at the roadside, stopping for a cuppa and chatting with the villagers.

I know the reality was it was genuinely traumatic at times, and a permanent clinic was always the aim so we could give much better patient care, but occasionally the nostalgia for those days kicks in!

The one thing I do worry we have lost from that time is a sense of really being out and about in the community. That by putting ourselves behind walls, we are isolating ourselves. Feeling we don't have as much direct contact with people is one of the reasons CNVRs are more important than ever. It reminds people that we are here, we want to play our part in the community, and we want to do our duty for the animals. It is so important to show people that we are here to help, that we are a presence, and they should think of us when a problem arises with a dog. We have continued to develop the CNVRs and have got them running like well-oiled machines now – with the odd spanner thrown in from time to time!

We aim to get as many of the CNVR days sponsored as possible, as the cost tends to be around £1,200 a day to cover all staff, equipment, petrol, treatments etc., so it is not a cheap task. Sponsorship might come through a grant from a charity such as Dogs Trust, or a local business, such as a hotel where the owners are keen to see the dogs treated in their area, but we are still having to cover many of the days ourselves.

We set up in the chosen open space, ideally with access to water and electricity, although we always bring a generator regardless, as you can't trust Sri Lankan electricity supplies not to go down.

We aim to do CNVRs over a minimum of three days at a time, and see seventy dogs in a day, which generally breaks down as forty street dogs, and thirty members of the public bringing us their own dogs. We use two trucks and a couple of teams made up of local dog catchers, who work for us part time, will go around in them aiming to pick up fifteen dogs at a time. They drive around looking for any that don't have the telltale sign that they have been neutered – the corner of their right ear cut – as well as any that look in need of medical care. Then they will net them and bring them back to our central point, where the vets and nurses are waiting. After that it becomes like a bit of a conveyor belt of neutering and vaccinating, although we do our best to spend any quality time we can with the dog too.

We see a CNVR day as precious time with an animal that we are only going to see potentially once in their life, so we will try and spoil them, and spend time in the recovery area, cuddling them, and trying to minimise any sense of stress. The last thing I want is for them to leave feeling the time they have spent with us is traumatic.

We register each dog with a number and area code for exactly where they were picked up, which is so important, to be sure they go back to their own territory. Then they get a pre-op check, so a full check of things like the dog's heart rate, mucus membranes, and a feel of the abdomen to make sure there are no obvious problems, before they are pre-medicated. Then they are laid out on tables and constantly monitored by nurses who are watching their jaw tone, heart rate, respiratory rate, eye position, temperatures – everything to make sure that there are no signs of distress.

Neutering is a sensitive operation, but the actual task, if done properly, can take literally minutes. It is more the recovery period from the anaesthetic that means dogs are kept in for longer. This is the riskiest part, and the nurses continue to monitor the dogs very closely during this time.

While we are working on the first set of dogs, the trucks go out for a second collection. Over time, because dogs are such savvy creatures, they have come to recognise dog catchers and avoid them. They have seen other dogs getting scooped up, and recognise the sight or smell of the van, as well as a man with a net, and will bark to warn each other away. Poor things have no idea that it is for their own good, and just see it that they are evading capture!

The other issue that can come up for the catchers is people who are anti-neutering. Over the years, most people have embraced the advantages of it, and understand that it is the most humane and sustainable way to reduce the number of unwanted dogs. It is also the fairest thing for these poor bitches who pop out a litter and are pregnant again almost instantly. Their bodies look worn out with large, dangling teats.

But there is still the occasional person who sees it as wrong, or a sin. They will suddenly pretend a street dog is theirs and block them from being taken. All we can do is try and reason, but occasionally getting the other fourteen dogs down to the CNVR site is more important than an hour spent arguing over the one. Allowing a dog to slip under the radar never sits well with me though.

Vaccination wise, we do rabies and what we call DHLPP, which covers them for distemper, hepatitis, leptospirosis, parainfluenza and parvovirus. They are also checked over for ticks, fleas and mange, and given a worming tablet if need be.

Then we pop a red collar on them before they go back out, so we know we have treated them, and it lets people know they have had their rabies vaccines, so can hopefully be reassuring. It also allows us to go back into the community and do post-CNVR counts, so we can keep an eye on the number of dogs in the area, and the percentage that we have treated. With adult dogs, the collars have a buckle, but with puppies it is Velcro. That way, as they grow, it doesn't start to strangle them, but will pop off when it gets too tight.

Inevitably our in-hospital patient numbers swell at these CNVRs, as it becomes apparent that some dogs need more treatment than just neutering and vaccination. Those ones are sent back to the clinic to be treated by the veterinary team not involved in the day.

They are the craziest days that we get through just on adrenaline, as well as dancing to good tunes while we work!

Typically we start at about five-thirty a.m. and end at eight p.m. or later, and while three days is our minimum, we aim to do at least five days at a time, and have even done up to ten, so it is a case of home to wind down and grab a few hours' sleep, before getting up to do it all over again.

We did five days in a row up in Arugam Bay on the east coast, when one kindly traveller raised enough funds for us to be there for that length of time, as well as for the treatment of those we had to take back to Gandara.

It is mentally and emotionally draining, but you know that in the long term this is easily one of the most productive days. The number of unwanted dogs will be reduced, those that there are will be healthier, and both of these benefits can only contribute to the locals viewing them in a better light, and having a kinder relationship with them.

I've always been adamant not to shy away from the dodgier areas, as too often these are the places that get ignored and people end up feeling resentful. In one of these, a man brought a cat along in a sack for treatment. When he opened it to show me, the cat ran off, and he angrily pulled a knife and came at me, claiming it was my fault. Luckily, the local staff jumped in, grabbed him, and told him to get out of there. He seemed drunk and angry, but fortunately he headed on his way and the rest of the day was calmer.

These are the places where the villagers take a bit of time to warm to you, but then never forget you, and when we returned there at a later date people were running over smiling and calling 'Dr Janey!' and bringing us cups of tea.

One of my favourite moments was going back for a CNVR in Nilwella, a few years on from our first one there, with my own team. Remember the child who had come every day on our first visit, and was looking after the street dogs, much to his neighbour's annoyance? I was in the middle of surgery this time when I looked up to see this same kid back and sat playing with the dogs. He was obviously much taller, but was still this brilliant, empathetic, natural with the dogs. It was really good to see him, and hopefully one day we will be able to get him a job in the clinic!

Another way we keep ourselves visible to people is through adoptions.

Adoption of the WECare dogs was no longer something that just happened thanks to word of mouth around the village, but had become much more structured ever since Jo had joined the team.

As the clinic became busier, the need to get the dogs adopted, sooner rather than later, became more apparent, but we had pretty much saturated the local area in terms of potential adopters. It was costing us more and more to keep feeding dogs who were actually back to full health, but couldn't go back on the streets for whatever reason, or were one of the growing number of puppies abandoned on our doorstep.

We had put out appeals for people to take one of the dogs on our social media sites previously, but Jo began to push this side, putting up posters of every available dog, to try and showcase them as individuals.

People will pop into the clinic and meet the dogs in the garden who are ready for adoption. Inevitably, the confident young ones go first, and dogs such as Tuts, who doesn't trust strangers and keeps her distance, end up staying. The adoptions lead to some great outcomes and I think it improves the lives of the people as well as the dogs.

Take Sandy, who was brought in to us as a little puppy with really bad skin. We treated it, and soon she was growing into a healthy, typical-looking brown Sri Lankan street dog. Being so young when she arrived meant she couldn't go back to the street, but needed an owner. To me she was gorgeous, but as she had no outstanding features, it took us a while to rehome her. There was always that fluffier, cuter or more unique pup waiting, whenever anyone came in looking to adopt.

Not that I minded, as she was such a lovely little character to have around the place. She was one of my favourite dogs to pass through the clinic, and radiated such a joy for life. Finally after five months this most amazing local family wanted to rehome her. They were one of the best adopters we have ever had, as they just loved her to bits, and although they were quite a poor family, they made sure that she was really well looked after. They would send us photos of Sandy as she settled in, even letting her sleep in their beds, which is practically unheard of in Sri Lanka. It really felt like a two-way relationship, where everyone's life was richer as a result of the adoption.

If we don't know the people on a personal level, we do a house check before a dog goes out, and then follow that up with visits down the line to see that everything is going well. We remember all our dogs and where they have gone, and when we are in the area with a spare moment, will pop in and see that they are happy.

Responsible dog ownership here is a very different thing to the UK. Realistically, the dog is only going to be around the home half the time as they will be off on their street adventures, so the important thing is they have a safe environment where they are fed, get a bed, have their freedom, and are offered a cuddle every now and then. It is about working out the genuine needs of these dogs, rather than what our impression is of what a dog needs.

We cannot be as stringent as in the UK – if we started insisting on a maximum number of hours the dog spent alone, or a minimum age for a child etc., it just wouldn't work. But our non-negotiable rules are that the owner doesn't live on a main road – remember it is puppies in particular we are rehoming and they are not street savvy – and no dog is to be kept on a chain or in a cage. If we can offer them a safer home than going back on the street, and they are ready to move on and make space for others in the clinic, we will do it.

It is also about having a gut feeling on the possible owners. Occasionally we have turned someone away as it just hasn't felt right, even though in theory they are ticking all the boxes, but people always seem to take it in their stride. And occasionally we have people who prove us wrong, bringing the dog back within days, complaining that it is a bit shy, or chewed their shoes. We explain that this is natural behaviour and suggest ways to cope, but sometimes we accept the match just wasn't right.

We also offer free health care for the dog for life, as the last thing I want is someone neglecting one of our puppies for financial reasons. I feel like we have a duty to those dogs for the rest of their lives, and offering that support can make it less intimidating for potential adopters.

Whenever she thought the adoptions weren't happening quickly enough, Jo would always say, 'People don't know they want a dog until they see one.' Then she would go off to a village with Chaminda and four puppies in the tuk-tuk, and talk to villagers about potentially adopting.

Some other charities think Sri Lankans don't like dogs and so rehoming is a waste of time. We don't agree. As repeatedly comes up, once you have addressed the reason for a person's concerns or fears, it turns out a lot of people can learn to really love dogs.

We also started running adoption days. This meant setting up pens in an area with the available dogs and getting people to come and meet the puppies and talk to us to see if rehoming a dog might be for them.

It is also a great opportunity for community interaction, and again we don't miss the education potential, but will sit in the pens with the dogs, kissing, cuddling and playing with them as they charge around. We had a great one on Matara beach front where people passing on the road and beach could see what we were doing and came over, loving all the puppies. It tends to draw out the real animal lovers of the area.

My absolute favourite was a lady who came to an adoption

day in Dikwella. She adopted a puppy, and shortly after I saw her putting her pup on a roundabout seat and really slowly pushing her, while busily talking away to her new friend. It was the sweetest moment, and so reassuring that the right person had adopted that dog that day.

Quite quickly, the number of dogs we had found homes for rose into the hundreds. Now that was a good feeling!

• CHAPTER TWENTY-FOUR •

THE DOGS WHO CHECK THEMSELVES IN

As I switched my scooter off outside the clinic one morning I glanced at the doorstep to see a bag, moving around of its own accord. Sighing, I peeped inside and, sure enough, there were three tiny cream puppies, just about old enough to open their eyes.

It had become one of the downsides of our growing reputation, we were seen as an easy place to leave unwanted pups.

Part of me was happy that these dogs weren't being killed or dumped somewhere they had no chance to fend for themselves, but the other part knew we couldn't afford to keep taking them on. Looking at these three I could see there was nothing wrong with them other than an owner not wanting them. 'Bloody well spay your dog!' I muttered in frustration.

Looking after puppies is an expensive and time-consuming business. Their milk costs us a fortune, but they need to be kept on it for about six weeks before they are weaned on to solid food. They need to be fed the milk every two to four hours, so nurses are up through the night feeding them. And no matter the expertise, nothing is as good as what the mum would do for the pup, and sadly lots of them don't end up surviving, so all round it is very hard.

Happily the law had been changed in 2017 to allow prosecution of anyone dumping a dog. They could face up to two years in prison and a 25,000 rupees fine (£120), although I am yet to see it making a real difference.

We had installed CCTV outside the clinic for security reasons, but also so that we could now potentially identify the people doing this dumping.

We were at bursting point already, but I scooped these three cuties up. There was nothing for it but to let them join the WECare gang, until we could rehome them.

Most dogs such as these make it to our doorstep thanks to humans, but some have taken matters into their own paws.

One day we were sat in the clinic office chatting, one eye on the CCTV camera, when we spotted a movement by the bins. What on earth was it? As we watched, we could make out a dog lying curled up in a ball, tucked in behind the bins. Maybe he was fine, but he didn't look like one of the regulars who pop by to see us, so it was definitely worth checking it out.

We went out and gasped in horror. This poor white and tan dog was hiding by the containers with the most horrendous bright pink burn down his back, with pretty much no skin on there right from his neck to his tail. It was clear someone had thrown boiling water over him, and then left him to suffer in this most agonising way. I was so sad for him, and so angry at the sick person who could do something like that.

The one lovely bit of it, though, was that looking back at the footage, he had walked himself right up to the clinic almost as though he knew this was the one place he could get fixed. We always say he was basically checking himself in!

None of us had ever seen him before, but we named him Chance, and got to work. The poor boy had third-degree burns to over 30 per cent of his body, and was in such a state. It was so extreme I don't believe he would have survived if he had ended up at any other vets in the area. It wasn't just a skin issue, but a systematic issue, i.e. it affected the whole body. Chance could have gone into shock at any time, and needed very careful management. Vets here are not cut out for that. It would be like taking a child with severe burns to the GP rather than A&E.

It took a lot of work over a long period, combined with so much love and TLC, but eventually he looked great. The scar healed well, his hair grew back everywhere, and he looked perfect. It was time for him to move on and find a home.

Before we could make a plan of action for him though, he was walking to the shop with Jo one day when another dog chased Chance and he ran off. We didn't see him for ages and were worried about where he had ended up. But we had to remember, this was a dog who had known how to find the clinic to help him in the first place, so we should have known he was fine. He had made himself at home in a house in the village where they loved him to bits. When we found out, we called around to see his new owners, and showed them a video of the way Chance had appeared with us. They couldn't believe his transformation. He is a different dog now, so happy, funny and healthy, and always trots over to say hello when I spot him in the village.

There are times when I am walking through Gandara or Talalla that I start to feel a bit like the Pied Piper. There are now so many dogs in the area that I have treated or spent time with, and they all come over to say hi, that I can be walking down the road with a dozen of them trotting behind. One day I will get a drone to follow me, and entertain you all!

Although Chance's check-in was as good as it gets, it does sometimes feel that dogs are destined to make it to us for treatment. Like somehow they know to come and find us when they are in need, although how that could happen, I've no idea. Take Troy. I was on my scooter going through Gandara one lunchtime, when I saw a dog I'd not seen before. I was studying him, thinking, 'Who are you?' and as I passed I could see a massive hole in the side of his head behind his ear. Shit! I pulled up and stood in front of him. Troy was walking with his head down and just kept going until he went straight into me. Then he looked up, and lay down in front of me. It was weird, like he just knew I was there to help him. He was in such a bad way, I was worried it was too late for him.

Troy was a decent-sized boy, though, so I couldn't get him on my scooter, and with the wound absolutely riddled with maggots, of course no tuk-tuk would take him, so I called Chaz and waited.

Once back at the hospital it was the usual maggot extraction mission before I could inspect the extent of the damage. The little critters were in so deep and the wound was so full-on, I was amazed they hadn't made it through to his brain, but it seems he had made it to us just in time. Troy had a good sleep the rest of that day, and the next we got the rest of the maggots out, before he jumped off the table and trotted round after me for the day. I couldn't believe it. Twenty-four hours before I really thought he was a gonner, and already his attitude was like, 'Oh yeah, see that hole in my head? Whatevs, I'll be fine.'

Troy was one of the friendliest dogs I have ever met, and he didn't want to let me out of his sight. He wasn't as friendly with other dogs though. In fact, he made it pretty clear they weren't to come near him. But the issues seemed to be more that he didn't want them near me – he had decided I was his!

Once the wound had recovered sufficiently, it was surgery time, and we were able to stitch up the hole and watch him carry on healing, before we took him back to the street where we found him. I've never seen him since, so I assume he headed back to where he was originally from, and what led him over to find me to get fixed up in the first place will always remain a mystery.

I've no idea what the locals think of me these days. Hopefully they understand why I am here now, and know that I have the best interests of the dogs and the country at heart. They certainly see me as part of the local community now and look out for me, even if they sometimes still look bemused at some of my antics. On a daily basis I seem to prove their thinking that I am a little bit crazy, and certainly did when it came to Cracker.

We have the screen that shows all our CCTV camera images up in the office, and people keep an eye on it throughout the day. One of the staff glanced up at one point to see this brown dog running past the clinic. She was convinced he had a wound on him, and as we were putting our noses out the front to see if there was any sign of him, a guy on a tractor came to get us. 'There is an injured dog; he is two doors down at this house.'

I walked up to the house and someone said that he was in a shed, asleep, so I assumed he was their dog, and it was all very relaxed. I went in and saw him in the corner, but when I approached him he went nuts. Ah okay, muzzle needed! I ran back to the clinic for a muzzle and lead, and went back to find they had him pinned up against the shed using a gate. They were leaning so hard he was practically in the gate, so my first thought was they were using too much force and his leg was about to snap, so I yelled at them to take it off him. Oops. I hadn't thought that one through. He was out of there like a shot.

I cursed myself for not having put a lead on him quickly before they removed the gate, especially as it was becoming clear he wasn't their dog, but a random street dog who had just ended up in their garden. No wonder he hadn't been so friendly when a whole group of people were trying to corner him in what he thought was a safe hideout.

He wasn't going to get away that easily, though, and I ran off after him. It was the middle of a hot day, but I had dressed for the air conditioning of the clinic, so was in jeans and a T-shirt. Great. I jogged along keeping pace with Cracker, as he was to eventually be named. He wasn't so scared that he was shooting off ahead of me, in fact he let me run alongside him at times, but he always made sure there was enough distance between us that I couldn't grab him. The sweat was dripping off me as we wound along the country roads up into more jungle-esque areas, and towards the house where some of the volunteers were living. I wasn't sure how long I could keep this up, but I also am not one to give up!

A random guy in a car pulled alongside me and asked if I needed help. It was a good example of the village community helping out, so I didn't worry that he was a stranger. Instead I had other concerns!

'Do you have air conditioning?' I gasped.

'Yes.'

So in I jumped. The guy kept up with the dog while I tried to tempt him over with food. No luck, so I called Sachira to come with a net. Then suddenly Cracker spotted a building site on the right and zip! He was off into it.

In typical lucky fashion, that was the point Sachira and Babi, two of the staff members from the clinic, turned up.

'He's in here, we just have to find him!' I tried to convince them, stumbling out into the jungle area, calling reassuring phrases to the dog.

Sachira and Babi just stared at me in shock. I had never been so sweaty in my life, and I don't think they knew whether to laugh, bundle me into the van back to the clinic, or go along with it. Quietly they took the latter option for a few minutes until it was clear Cracker had cleared out.

'He was there, I am so sorry,' I muttered, laughing, embarrassed and annoyed all in one. There was nothing for it but to head back to the clinic.

For the next few days we kept an eye out for him, and it was like he was tormenting us. Emily went on a similar wild-goose chase when he ran past her outside the clinic, again with no luck. Everyone locally knew we were looking for him and were to keep us posted if he appeared. I also made it clear if he came back to sleep in the neighbour's shed, I wouldn't be so stupid about giving him an inch this time, but would have him caught straight away.

Five days later, though, I was due to head to Dubai for a work stint, and we still didn't have him. It was bugging me as I jumped into a car to the airport, all clean and fresh, ready for the flight in a little dungaree dress and white T-shirt. I didn't like to think of him suffering, and knew the longer he was out there untreated, the worse it would get. I didn't want him to die, just because I had messed up that first chance to catch him.

As we passed through Gandara, who did I spot, but Cracker! 'Stop the car!' I yelled, and that was it, I was off legging it down the main road after him.

He hadn't spotted me, and as he headed past the petrol station he stopped to sniff something, and that was my moment. I grabbed him, not caring whether he turned and bit me or not. I had him!

Instead though he turned his head and looked at me, as if to say, 'Oh all right then, you've got me, we've had fun on this chase though, haven't we?'

No we bloody haven't, Cracker!

There was no chance of me being allowed back in this posh

car with a dog who was covered in stinking maggot juice, as was I now from holding him. I stood there holding him and trying to figure out what to do next. My friend called Chaminda to get him to come down and collect me, but as the minutes ticked by, I was getting later for my flight.

It seemed half the village were standing around just looking at me as I stood holding this dog, and the other local dogs, confused at what was going on, were coming over barking. Come on ground, swallow me whole! It was the middle of yet another super-hot day, and I was sweating and trying to get just one mouthful of fresh air away from the maggot juice smell. If you haven't smelt it before, it is so hard to describe. It is the worst smell in the world, and really lingers in your nostrils. It honestly is reminiscent of death …

Just as I was thinking maybe I could try walking Cracker back to the clinic (realistically it wasn't that far), I spotted a tuk-tuk guy looking at me with a crumb of pity. 'Please?' I said, giving him my biggest, hopeful smile.

And what a legend, he swung his tuk-tuk around and signalled at me to hop in. I held Cracker partly out of the tuk-tuk to try and show my respect and appreciation to the guy. Then as we pulled up at the clinic at the same time as Chaminda, it turned out they knew each other.

As I thanked him he was saying in Sinhalese to Chaminda that he could just see the dog was in pain and he couldn't not help. It was so nice to hear that when everyone else had just been shaking their heads and driving past.

'I've got Cracker!' I called to Emily.

'Yay!'

'I'm covered in maggot juice and I'm really late to the airport!'

'Oooooh.'

I dashed off, leaving him in her capable hands, and just about made my flight, but I'm sure I nearly cleared the plane with the smell. I hadn't managed to change, and all journey I just kept getting whiffs of this vile smell drifting off me. Who knows what everyone around me thought.

Arriving at my friend's house in Dubai where I was staying, her first question was, 'Ooh, what is that stink?'

'Yep, it is me. Definitely me … '

But that is WECare life, never a calm moment, and certainly never with things happening how, when, and the way you want them to.

Cracker made a great recovery and was released in early 2019. I don't think he was a particularly local dog, as it turned out people had seen him in all sorts of villages, quite far afield, almost as if he had been doing loops to find the clinic – even if he was too afraid to come in once he was there!

Then, as well as the dogs who check themselves in, you get the dogs who just won't leave …

Take Jeremy. Jezza was picked up at a neutering clinic in Tangalle – a town about twenty kilometres along the coast from us. He was a super-friendly, well-built, white dog, but his skin was in the most awful state, so as well as all the usual CNVR treatment, we brought him back to the clinic for four weeks of skin treatment. A bit like Mali, he had obviously been suffering from mange, ticks and lice for a really long time, and some of the damage to his skin was going to be permanent. But we did what we could, and he was still a darn sight better looking and, crucially, more comfortable, by the time we drove him back to his home to catch up with all his mates.

The end of our Jezza? Not a chance. The next day I got to work, and who was there sat outside the gate? Jeremy, of course. There was a small chance that someone had picked him up and dumped him outside the clinic, thinking he needed treatment, as despite our best efforts his hair was still sparse, and it is difficult to think of him as healthy looking. It wasn't likely, but we gave him another lift back to Tangalle.

Only the next day, of course, he was back again. So we drove him to his home ... and he came back. That was it, I gave up. It was clear he loved us more than his friends, and who am I to say he is wrong?! It was impressive dedication really. The lovely lad would have had to walk those twenty kilometres along busy roads, passing through territory belonging to hundreds of other dogs, and he had pulled it off not once, but three times. So now he officially lives in Gandara and is often found waiting outside the clinic for cuddles and love. It's the most commitment I've had from a guy in a long time!

CHAPTER TWENTY-FIVE

THE TOUGHEST SURGERIES

Surgery is my favourite part of being a vet. I love the challenge of overcoming all sorts of difficulties, the time pressure, and the instant changes you can make to a dog's health.

Equally I try and keep an upbeat vibe to the room, so it doesn't get too intense, with music playing and me singing along (badly).

At times I need to focus, but when things are more straightforward – say neutering – I will chat away to the nurses and those helping out in surgery. As well as Emily and the local lads, we took on a great Sri Lankan lady called Thushari.

Thushari came knocking on our door one day asking if we would like to hire her, as she used to work at a vets in Colombo. Err, yes! She moved to the area with her husband's job, and we were so lucky that she came to us. She is such a hard worker and has a really positive attitude. She gets up every day at four a.m. to cook from scratch and sort the family home out, before coming to work for us as an animal care assistant. Her husband is really supportive of her and what we do, and she's been a real asset to WECare. Veterinary nursing isn't a recognised qualification in Sri Lanka yet, but I am looking into ways we can help to change this, and maybe help people qualify while working for us. If this happens, Thushari will be top of my list.

Since being here I've become much less precious about having the exact equipment I want for surgery – I've had to, to get by. I'm not talking about anything that compromises the surgery; we are one of the best-equipped clinics on the island, and the aim is to raise standards, not cut corners, but we just don't have access or funds for everything I'd like. So that might mean using a clamp smaller than one I'd prefer, or a product that feels old-fashioned. Since my university days I've liked to be up to speed on veterinary developments, but here I am improvising, and just happy to have supplies. For example, remember how I said people were using nylon for ligatures when I arrived, to tie knots in the abdomen, around the uterus, etc.? To me that is disgusting and can cause adhesions, so we introduced catgut. Well, in the UK now this is seen as outdated, because while it is absorbable, it is a natural product so you can't predict how long it will take to dissolve. It is still seen as a completely acceptable product, but vets in the UK are now moving over to using Vicryl. It does the same job, but it is synthetic, and has been tested to the nth degree, so you can tell exactly how long it is going to last.

In the past I would have wanted to switch our clinic over to Vicryl, but the reality is we have never had an issue with catgut. It is cheaper, and everyone here is now trained up to use that instead of nylon, so I don't want to start introducing something different yet. You have to tie the knots in a different way etc., and I don't want to start getting post-op complications. However, I have started using Vicryl or Monocryl for sutures. I want to constantly strive for a higher standard so sutures are a good place to start introducing the Vicryl.

My biggest obsession is surgical blades. You can get cheap ones or you can get good ones. And there is nothing worse than going into surgery and the blade isn't cutting as well or as cleanly as you like. I refuse to try and save money on those, as it is not worth it.

It would be fair to say that my surgery has improved tenfold while being here. That is not meant in an arrogant way, but is a natural progression of everything I've had to learn and get better at, because of the conditions we are working in. There are several surgeries that stand out to me for a mix of reasons, everything from pride to heartbreak.

Some of the most fiddly surgeries have been tumour removal. A lovely hairless chap called Dobby came in with a mass on his forehead and across his right eye that had obviously been there for a while. The poor dog must have been in lots of pain, and found it so irritating. How can people have seen him like that every day, and not told someone?

I wanted to find out what I was working with, so I took a section of the mass and sent it off to the lab for testing. Normally you would expect to get a report back with a breakdown of the tumour type, such as a mast cell tumour, soft tissue sarcoma, squamous cell carcinoma, etc. But this one just came back 'cancer cells'. Not helpful! There is a different chemo protocol for each type, so that was really annoying.

In the end I opted just to go for surgery, although I did think it was going to be almost impossible to remove the whole tumour, thanks to its positioning. However, with some careful work, I'm chuffed to say I managed it, although I couldn't get very good margins, so I am fearful of it coming back. If that happens, we will deal with it down the line, but for now we know we did our best and extended his life. This time when he went back to his home on the streets, we made sure he had a guardian who could contact us as soon as anything started to go wrong. No more suffering in silence for Dobby.

Then there are the tumours that are there thanks to sex, as it's not just humans who can get some pretty grotty physical issues without protection, but dogs too. TVT (transmissible venereal tumour) is a sexually transmitted cancer, i.e. it is passed on from dog to dog through the transfer of live cancer cells, normally during mating. It looks like a red/pink cauliflower kind of lump on a dog's penis or vulva, and is a really shocking sight if you have never seen it before. It is so awful and uncomfortable for a dog.

It isn't just transferred through sex either. If a dog even sniffs or licks the infected area of a dog, he or she can catch a TVT on their nose and around their head. Then it ends up looking like this huge open sore, and can cause swelling and nose bleeds. It is not a pretty sight.

It can occasionally be fatal, but is also easily treated with a run of chemotherapy sessions over a month or two. In a handful of cases, though, I have had to use surgery instead to tackle it.

It is the positioning of the TVT that determines just how hard the surgery is, which was certainly true of poor Walter, who got a tumour on his penis that was so big it pretty much blocked his ability to pee. A beautiful tan and white dog, he was found on the beach in Tangalle and I swear that tumour was nearly as big as my head. Walter had this brilliant way of looking at you with a suspicious gaze, as though he knew you were about to get too close for comfort with his privates. We treated it repeatedly with chemo, and he responded well, but it was so huge that it didn't totally reduce.

In the end it was clear I had to operate, and it was going to be one of the hardest surgeries I had done in a while. The tumour was so big it had engulfed his whole penis – I literally couldn't even see where the tumour ended and his penis began.

It was crucial for me to avoid the urethra, which ran right through the middle, and the slightest slip or error could have proved very problematic. So it was tough, but I was able to reconstruct Walter's penis and send him on his way. We still get updates on him from locals now, and he is apparently able to mark his territory all over Tangalle without any difficulty!

Having a TVT is a serious enough issue for a dog that on a rare night when I was off to see a band, and spotted a dog with a tumour, I wasn't prepared to wait until the next day to go back and try and find her. I was in the tuk-tuk with friends, nearly at the venue and half an hour from the clinic, when I spotted the black dog in the dark down an alleyway. My mates couldn't believe I had clocked her as we whizzed past, but I've definitely developed a sixth sense for pups in need. We scooped her up and round we turned to the hospital – an hour's round trip – then headed back off to the party. We'd missed most of the band's set, but you can't really choose that over saving a life, can you? And therein lies the story of my life (or lack of social life, at least).

It was a huge learning curve for me to learn about TVTs, as thankfully they don't exist in the UK. It was one of those that we had touched on at university, but I had to pretty much read up on it from scratch when I first came across it, as well as working out the best ways for me to treat it. You can't vaccinate against it, but it disappeared in the twentieth century, as the number of feral dogs reduced, and neutering became an accepted practice. It boils down to the fact our dogs in the UK aren't running around shagging each other all the time, like the randy bunch in Sri Lanka!

The most intricate surgery of my life was on a dog called Liquorice. She had been hit by a car and come in with a broken leg, and everything appeared to be straightforward. She spent a few weeks recovering well, and it seemed like it wouldn't be long until she was back home on the streets.

This was January 2019, and I wasn't in the clinic much at that time as I had caught a virus and kept fainting, even when I was lying in bed. I had taken a few weeks out to try and recover, but I was weak. But then this dog, who had shown no signs of respiratory problems up until now, started struggling to breathe. Everything I was hearing from the guys in the clinic sounded worrying so I forced myself out of bed to go in and have a look. I checked Liquorice over and started to suspect that she might have a diaphragmatic hernia. This means that a patient's diaphragm has ruptured, and one of their organs has moved up into the chest. In this case the RTA that had broken her leg could easily have damaged her diaphragm, and I was worried it was her liver that had become displaced. In the UK it would be simple to determine if this was the case through a quick X-ray, but of course we didn't have that luxury.

If what I was suspecting turned out to be true, Liquorice was at potential risk of death, and it was vital we dealt with it as soon as possible. There was nothing for it, but to go into surgery to see what we were dealing with, and pray it was a false alarm. But things never turn out as you want, do they?

Opening Liquorice up, I could instantly see that not only had her liver moved up into her chest cavity, but that it was fused to her lung lobe, which meant it had probably been there ever since the accident. A real disaster, and really tough to deal with from a vet's point of view.

Without the fusing, it can be fiddly, as you have to pull everything out of the chest and basically rearrange it back to where it should be, then close everything up again. But with these two fused, it was a very different story. You do not want a liver to bleed and you don't want to puncture a lung, so there was no room for even the tiniest slip while getting them apart.

I felt shaky even just standing up, but knew there was no time to waste and I was the only person available who had done surgery of this sort before. There was nothing for it but to get started.

It was all about going slowly and patiently, and not losing focus, as I worked on each individual section. A mass removal can have the same slow, painstaking feel to it, but this was harder as I was working blind most of the time. The surgery was in the chest, but I was coming at it from the abdomen, so only had a tiny amount of visual help, and was mostly doing it by feel. I didn't even want to take a moment to step away and stretch. It was relentless.

A few times I felt like I was going to pass out, and one of the nurses kept feeding me Coca-Cola to ensure I didn't faint into the dog's abdomen! But steadily and surely it all worked and Liquorice was doing good. I was using every ounce of my reserve to keep going and get through this. We had spent a month fixing up her leg, we were going to get this little girl back out there to live life.

After three hours, I was there. Everything was separated and back where it should be, and I was closing her back up. But, as I literally placed the last suture, she crashed. We tried everything but there was no waking her up. She was gone.

That was the hardest surgery I had ever done, and I'd done it bloody well, so to get to that point and lose her, it was heartbreaking. Why couldn't you have clung on just a bit longer, Liquorice, and you would have been home and clear?

It was so hard for everyone in the hospital. That morning they had seen what seemed like a relatively healthy dog, who had been recovering and wriggling her lovely little self into everyone's heart, and then I took her to theatre, and now she was dead.

Seeing Thushari in tears was horrible. Although I knew I had put my all into it, and couldn't have done anything differently, you still end up with a feeling of responsibility, and it can knock your confidence for a bit.

Add that to the fact I was still feeling so ill, and for the next few weeks I shook every time I carried out surgery. It was weird. I know some people shake every time they carry out surgery, maybe from the pressure of people watching, but it is not me. It got so bad that people actually commented on it at the next CNVR. I think I was just feeling so fragile, and couldn't pull myself back together 100 per cent. Luckily, things picked back up, and by the next month my steady, confident surgery hands had returned.

There was one dog who really broke my heart, and whose case feels as fresh today as it did at the time. Remember Sandy, the pup who had a happy outcome of adoption with the best family?

Well, one morning I was lying in bed writing my to-do list for another day in the clinic, when Chaminda called. It was six a.m., so this was really unusual.

'Dr Janey, there is an emergency with Sandy.'

I was out of bed and off to the clinic like a shot, imagining I might be arriving to a broken leg. Poor pup was just out of the wars and now back in trouble. But nothing could have prepared me for what I was about to see.

I peered into the big laundry tub that had been used to carry Sandy in, and all I could focus on were her intestines. There was a hole in her abdomen, and all her guts were hanging out. Another dog had come on to their property and Sandy had chased him off, but had then been hit by a car. She just lay there looking up at me with these confused but trusting eyes, and my heart almost broke on the spot.

There was no time to be soft. We went straight into emergency surgery. I removed fifteen centimetres of gut trying to save what I could, but there was a lot of contamination from the amount of grit and dirt, and I was worried that we were going to be facing postoperative complications such as peritonitis.

Sandy stayed stable throughout the anaesthetic, apart from a low temperature, which is common in longer surgeries, so we were trying to manage that. She was doing so well, it felt perfect – or as perfect as it could be in this scenario.

I sighed with relief when I told the nurses we could bring her round. She woke up, and after a few minutes I carried her through into the prep room like a baby. As I kissed her she looked at me, and I put her in the kennel. But then suddenly she stopped breathing.

We retubed her and started breathing for her, but then her heart stopped too. The chances of getting a dog back once they have crashed are less than 10 per cent.

I pumped Sandy's chest and we used Adrenalin, and her heart started up again, but we were still having to breathe for her.

Over the next two hours she crashed twice more, her heart restarting as I pumped her chest, crying. It was one of the few times my emotions spilled out in surgery, but she was like one of our babies. I was determined to get her back, and was thinking desperately of anything else I could try. We were willing her to take each breath on her own. It was absolute agony.

Sandy had grown up at the hospital and I was so attached to her, and she had just found her happy-ever-after. This was like that *Final Destination* situation all over again, with death stalking a young dog who didn't deserve it. Everything about it was so unfair.

A vet with thirteen years' experience was over volunteering from the UK at the time and she couldn't see any other route we could take either. But it was really hard to accept that it was out of our hands.

In the end, when she crashed for a third time, I decided we needed to let her go. It was the saddest and worst case of my life, and even writing this is making me teary. It all still feels so fresh. And of course her new family were heartbroken. I spent ages thinking what I could have done differently, even questioning the way I had carried her through to her kennel, but it was silly, the answer was nothing. In reality I know we went above and beyond. Even had that been in the UK, it would have been the best care she could have received. It was just so hard to accept. It was such shitty, unfair timing. Sandy had found her new perfect life, only to have it snatched away from her.

I have a little tear for most dogs we lose, although it isn't always the obvious ones – some cases just get me for whatever reason. I think if their death seems particularly unfair I find it hardest. Only recently I was sobbing while putting down Stella, a dog who had been with us for a month. I didn't even know her that well, but she hadn't enjoyed her time in the hospital and had been really unhappy, so there was something about that which got to me. At least with most of them you think, well, their last month was pain free and happy. Most dogs accept and adapt to the temporary set-up, but occasionally there is one who will get very stressed by it, no matter what you do. As this was the case with Stella, I felt so sad for her.

I don't think crying makes me a bad vet. Lots of people say you shouldn't do it, but I've never tried to fight it. Other times for my own peace of mind I have to switch off my emotions to get through a day. I worry if people don't know me, it looks like I breeze into the clinic, 'Oh we need to put Jaegar (or whoever) to sleep today,' then I head back out of the room. It's not that I don't care, but sometimes I just need to distance myself for my own sanity. Anyone who thinks they are going into a career as a vet for simple days of playing with fluffy animals is in for a real shock. Difficult life or death decisions are unfortunately par for the course.

CHAPTER TWENTY-SIX

THE R WORD

If there is one word that sends fear through the heart of any locals or tourists, it is the dreaded 'rabies'.

It is understandable really, as there is no escaping the fact it is a pretty grim disease that kills 55,000 humans worldwide each year, although only around one hundred of these deaths are in Sri Lanka. Pretty much everyone who catches it will die from it in unpleasant circumstances if they don't receive any treatment. The same applies to dogs – death is a guarantee. The typical symptoms for a human start with a headache and temperature, then it rapidly escalates to aggression, foaming at the mouth, confusion, hallucinations, and then finally paralysis. Doesn't sound a great way to go, does it?

It is an infectious viral disease, and while animals such as bats, monkeys, foxes and cats can all carry it, 99 per cent of the time if a human has been infected, it has come via a dog. It is spread by the saliva of an infected animal, generally via a bite.

But that still doesn't mean every dog has it. In fact, only a very small percentage of dogs in Sri Lanka do, and even that has been rapidly falling ever since CNVRs were introduced. But the disease is so feared by many Sri Lankans that they treat all dogs as if they have it. This can range from just avoiding them, right through to taking measures to kill them. It is one of the reasons we have struggled so hard with finding local staff, and getting people on board with us.

It is also one of the first things most volunteers ask about, and we strongly advise that everyone gets their rabies vaccinations before coming out to join us. It is a pre-exposure vaccine, so it doesn't actually give you immunity, but it buys you time. You need to go for two to three more doses of the vaccine if you could have been exposed to the disease. In a perfect world this should be once on the day of the bite, with a second three days later. The pre-exposure vaccine has helped your body develop antibodies to fight off rabies, but if you do get infected these antibodies need a boost to make sure they can stop the disease spreading.

The reality was, aware though I was of the existence of rabies in Sri Lanka, for the first three years I didn't see any sign of it at all, so the risk seemed low. But nevertheless, initially whenever I got a bite that drew blood, I would go for the post-exposure treatment. I rarely get serious bites – in fact, I think the only one was Jimmy, that time he was frustrated at having his dressing changed when there were monkeys he could be catching – but I took nicks just as seriously. Stressed or frightened dogs can give a warning snap, and while they don't really cause any damage or particularly hurt, they occasionally draw a bit of blood.

The first four or five times that happened, I went and had my follow-up vaccinations in Matara, but the amount of this stuff that was getting pumped into my body started to feel a bit ridiculous. I don't need to get the post-exposure vaccinations now, as I have had so many. I had an antibody titer, which is a test to see my level of protection. It turns out I am a bit of a superwoman against rabies, as anything above two is a normal level – mine is one-hundred and eighty! The doctor actually said it would be dangerous for me to have any for a while.

Jo was also a regular at the hospital. It is almost like a right of passage of working at WECare. She was well known for getting tablets in the mouths of unwilling dogs, unafraid of giving it a go, knowing it would help them, but inevitably getting the occasional bite for her troubles.

We followed a strict procedure for all the dogs, initially keeping them quarantined from each other. While everyone imagines all rabid dogs to be going crazy and foaming at the mouth, this isn't the case, so just because I thought a dog seemed fine, there was no guarantee that they were. Unprovoked aggression is a clear sign as the disease develops, but rabies generally has an incubation period of one to two weeks, and potentially up to four or five weeks, so how is anyone to know if they have rabies in that period? There has even been some evidence of cases incubating for up to six months.

What makes it even trickier is you cannot classically test a living dog for rabies. There is a pre-mortem test that is emerging on to the market as I write, but until now the only accurate test has entailed testing brain tissue from two areas of the brain, and these cannot be accessed until an animal is dead.

You only have to vaccinate 70 per cent of a dog population to eradicate rabies, as it will break the cycle of transmission, and of course we had been doing this since the beginning, as getting rid of the disease was one of the ultimate goals. The vaccine is a single jab, and then the dog is covered for three years. We are so cautious here in Sri Lanka about doing everything we can to eradicate the disease, though, that if you can vaccinate dogs yearly, the hope is none of them slip under the radar. It felt to some degree like the strategy was working, as I just never saw rabies. And let's face it, it shouldn't be too tricky to get 70 per cent of the dogs, if only there were enough CNVRs happening around the country in one big blitz. I can but dream!

The human vaccine only costs around 600–1,000 rupees (£3–£5). Why would you not pay that if it could save your life? It is free for locals, so you will often see them in the hospital getting treatment for the slightest scratch.

But then things suddenly changed. In October 2017, reports started coming through of a French kid who had died of rabies after visiting Dikwella in the summer. Apparently the ten-year-old had been bitten by a street puppy, but the family hadn't been too concerned at the time, and went back to the Rhône Valley in France. Then a few weeks later he began showing symptoms, such as struggling to swallow, and they took him to hospital, but by then it was too late.

Dikwella is slap bang in our area, and my first thought was panic that all the local street dogs would be killed as a result. Although there is a no-kill policy in the country, I was sure this would be the perfect excuse for anyone who was anti street dogs to argue now was the time to make an exception. The growing tourism industry is hugely important to the country, so if they thought something like this could deter tourists, the government would be very keen to take action.

So I went to the Ministry of Health in Matara and Dikwella to see what could be done, and was very happy when I was told that the reports were false and the boy had been misdiagnosed. Sweet. No need to panic, high alert over, move on. I confidently told everyone we were in the clear, and that the result had been a false positive.

Except it wasn't. Just as we had forgotten about it and normal life had resumed, I got a message from someone from another organisation pointing me to an official French website with rabies results listed – the kid was confirmed as having had rabies. It was frustrating, as we now knew for sure there had been rabies within our area and, with the proper heads-up, we could have done some real damage limitation and gone all out on the vaccination programme.

The following summer when I was away from the clinic celebrating my thirtieth birthday, a CNVR was running in Mawella. The dog catchers had picked up a mum dog and her four puppies, who were around ten weeks old, and put them together in a crate. But mama dog was particularly agitated, which the catchers assumed came from a place of protectiveness for her pups, and a real dislike of being netted. But as she seemed so stressed, rather than spend time gathering up more dogs, they came straight back to the CNVR venue to drop them off.

Jo, as fearless as ever, took one look at how worked up she was, and dived straight in. She scooped her up and put her on the operating table so the vet could give her the anaesthetic straight away.

Hoping that as she and her kids came round from their operations things would be calmer, they were all put into the recovery area together, along with other dogs. But as she regained consciousness, it was clear mama dog seemed more grouchy and distressed, and began biting her own puppies.

Again Jo was in like a shot, and separated the squealing youngsters, but soon the angry mum had turned her attention to other dogs. Jo grabbed a net and caught her in it, but as she twisted it to secure her, she got a bite on her shin through the net for her troubles. At the time Jo was focused on calming the dog, and getting her in a state where she could be reunited with her puppies and put back to their home on the street. It was clear the situation was stressful for her, so the less time she had to spend in our care, the better.

The CNVR continued with less drama, but when the dog catchers dropped mum and babies back home, they came back to report that locals complained she had bitten other people in the area.

The next day DN called Jo in the evening to say she had attacked four more people that day, as well as six other dogs, and then promptly, shockingly, died. Shit. Suddenly rabies was in everyone's mind as a very real option.

Poor Jo, remembering the bite she had received, got herself straight off to hospital for her follow-up injections. There was confusion over the treatment she was offered, as it was different to the serum she had received on previous visits. Knowing there was a higher risk this time, it was particularly worrying for her, and we needed to make sure she felt confident that the treatment she was getting was right, by clarifying it with doctors. Having had the post-exposure treatment so many times, you almost get used to it, but it doesn't take away from the fact that it is bloody scary to think there is the tiniest chance you might be infected by rabies.

Meantime, as usual, the dogs were at the forefront of my mind.

We needed to get the puppies and the dogs that locals told us had been bitten, so we could isolate them before there was any chance of them spreading it further.

I couldn't stop thinking about the puppies who were without a mum, and now at a high risk of having contracted rabies too. It can be passed on through blood, saliva, or a mother's milk, and chances were the pups had probably been in contact with all three. If mama dog had it, I could be pretty damn sure the puppies did too.

A couple of the staff raced over to the village to get the mum dog's body, in the hope we could send it off for testing, but were frustrated to find the locals had already buried her. Understandably they wanted her out of the way as soon as possible, but it was irritating as even though every sign pointed towards her having rabies, we would never be able to know for certain.

We managed to round up the four puppies, but what to do now? There was no way to tell if these little guys were carriers while they were still alive and, unlike with humans, there is no post-exposure protocol for animals.

It was a horrible decision for me to have to make, and I took myself off alone for a rational think-through of the situation. Do we euthanise four potentially healthy puppies? Or do we risk keeping them alive and they turn out to be rabid? It was heartbreaking, but I had to go with rational thinking over emotion. Public health was my primary responsibility. I'd already called the local authorities to let them know what had happened.

'We have to put them to sleep,' I said eventually. 'It seems brutal, but it is the only sensible thing we can do.'

'Shall we send their heads off to the lab?' someone asked. We had done it a few times in the past with dogs, but I shook my head.

'I'd not be able to sleep at night if I knew we had just killed four innocent puppies. It won't change anything in practical terms, and will just make us feel even worse.'

I had a heavy heart at the end of that day. I was confident I had made the right decision, but it didn't make it any easier. It was like a necessary evil for the good of the dog population overall – and for humans – but those poor little pups had done nothing to deserve their fate.

This was all going on at the time I was suffering from general burn out, and trying to get myself back on track. As part of that I was due to go away one evening soon after to the east coast for a few days surfing so decided to cheer myself up with a quick local surf before I went. I jumped on the scooter with my board on the side rack and headed to Dikwella, spotting a pup charging along the side of the road on my way.

'If she is still there on my way back, I'll stop and check her out', I promised myself, thinking from the brief glimpse I'd got, that she looked a bit mangey.

Sure enough, as I headed back, this bald little pup was still wandering down the middle of the road, with a hot water burn behind her ear, and no other dog or owner in sight.

Parking up I headed towards her, bending down and holding out my hand and talking in my best reassuring tone. She came charging towards me – a confident one, easy! – and then promptly bit me.

What the hell? Pretty much any dog you come across in an open space will make the choice to go the other way if they are nervous or wary. They rarely choose fight when the flight option is right there for them to take.

Surprised, I followed her. The poor pup's skin looked so sore, there was no way I was prepared to leave her. Besides, she was such a tiny little thing, what harm could she do?

I tried again, and received another bite for my efforts, this time drawing blood.

I rang Emily at the clinic. 'Okay this is going to sound ridiculous, but I am in Dikwella with a puppy, and I can't catch it. Can you send Chaz with a towel and a box? It's like she is rabid!'

With Chaz's help I caught her, and got her in a box.

'Let me know if she dies in the next few days,' I said, laughing nervously, before heading off on my trip.

A bit of me must have thought deep down that rabies was a legitimate risk, especially so soon after the four puppies. But I guess making light of it was a coping mechanism, as no one really wants to think it's an option, do they? After four years on the island I couldn't really believe that I had just come across a rabid dog, and been bitten by it.

But just two days later I got the call. 'Janey, the dog has died.'

My heart sank. This was all turning into a nightmare. I couldn't fathom where these cases were coming from, and on a personal level I was now miles from any hospital with the follow-up vaccines. I had known deep down there was a chance it was rabies, but I guess I was willing it not to be. I headed to hospital and went on a drip and had the injections.

Back at the clinic they removed the puppy's head, put it in an ice box, and sent it off to Colombo to a lab for testing. The result came back – positive for rabies. This time there was no doubt.

Although it was what I had expected by then, it was still a shock. It was a stark reminder that we needed to tighten up on our procedures on that front. Rabies wasn't this mythical thing, but something we now knew 100 per cent was in a dog in our area that we had attempted to treat.

It is easier said than done, though, as in the moment when you are dealing with a dog, you are thinking about them rather than yourself.

Since then we have had one more rabies case. A dog came in struggling to walk, and the volunteer vet treating her assumed she was the latest in an endless line of dogs who had been hit by a vehicle.

She was worried about a jaw fracture so checked her mouth. It turned out the dog was actually suffering with flaccid paralysis (weak, reduced muscle ability) brought on by rabies. Unfortunately, the vet had some open cuts on her hands at the time, so was worried the saliva may well have come into contact with them during the jaw examination, so there was a risk she had contracted rabies, and she had to go and get her jabs too.

It has all been a real reminder that this disease is ever-present.

I don't trust any dog not to be carrying the disease, and it is far too horrible to take the risk. If they start showing the signs a week down the line and you have done nothing about it, it's too late, so we will always veer on this side of caution.

In late 2018 owners brought in a dog called Rosie, claiming she had been attacked by another dog, who had been really aggressive and crazy, and promptly died the next day.

Everything about that pointed towards a rabid dog, and the

course of action at that stage would sadly normally be to put the dog to sleep. But her only real injury was a broken elbow, which I knew was easily fixable, and it was possible we could keep her isolated for six months while we waited for any rabies to appear, or the time to pass. It seemed worth looking a bit further into this rabid dog, both for Rosie's sake, and for any other potential victims. We asked the owners for more details, and suddenly the story changed. And then changed again. Before they went back to the original version. Hmm.

I got one of our local workers to go and talk to other villagers where the dog came from, and he came back to say no one else had come across this rabid dog.

I had no idea what had gone on, but I was doubting the story more and more by the minute. And looking at Rosie's sweet hopeful face, I decided the only right thing to do was isolation over euthanasia. Yes, six months away from other dogs for such a sociable little lady was going to suck, but at least she would live. And anyhow as we all felt so sorry for her, she probably got more visits in her kennel and playtime than any other dog in those six months!

Sure enough, the period ended and she and her newly mended elbow moved out to live with the rest of the dogs in the garden, much to her excitement. We tried to contact her owners to let them know she was ready to go home, but it turned out they had given us false details. I can only now assume that they effectively wanted to dump her, and concocted the rabies story as part of that. Good of them to make Rosie spend six months in isolation, and to burden us with the extra costs that came with that.

Anyhow, it does show just how seriously we take any chance of rabies, and that we want to do all we can to prevent its spread.

I think about the fact I hadn't come across a single case in three years, then suddenly saw four cases in one year. We have vaccinated 7,000 dogs in the area, so where is it coming from? I think it is really down to the fact we are seeing so many more dogs, and people now bring them to us when they might have left them to die in the past, so maybe that increases the chances of us seeing one. I'd be lying if I said it wasn't a bit scary, but it is exactly why our vaccination programme is so crucial.

CHAPTER TWENTY-SEVEN

TACKLING THE TOURISTS

'Sri Lanka is the best country I have visited! The only thing I hated was seeing the state of the street dogs, and feeling helpless as I didn't know what I could do.'

Ah, how many times have I heard this line from tourists. If you aren't mentally prepared for what you will see, or even if you are, it can prove quite distressing.

I know this feeling all too well, as I was obviously one of those very tourists on my first visit. I sympathise with where these people are coming from. No one wants to see a dog in need, and find there is no help available. It is one of the core reasons I started WECare. Of course, the main one is to purely and simply give the dogs a better life, but also so that people aren't eaten up by being unable to help. It is important to me that those people don't spend their whole holiday suffering with a sense of helplessness, and that there are options available if they want to help. It is that inability to take action that can leave a visitor to the country feeling miserable. Often people have one particular dog they feel especially frustrated about, whether because they have become attached to it, or it is in a particularly bad way. They will go round in circles looking for a solution, and can become a bit obsessed with it, as I did with Tom and his cut eye on that first trip.

When tourism began to really take off in Sri Lanka, it actually began to backfire on the dogs. When people showed their evident distress at the number of stray dogs they were seeing around the place, those in the tourist industry took it to mean they didn't like them. The success of tourism was hugely important, so the tourist industry tried to get rid of the dogs by hiding them, displacing them, or even killing them. That really angered me, and I was talking to hotel and restaurant owners, trying to say, 'No! Tourists absolutely love seeing the dogs around, but we need to make sure they are healthy and happy. Then your street dogs can actually be a selling point. People actually love being surrounded by dogs.'

I don't like reducing a dog's well-being down to effectively acting as a financial carrot, but I understood the fear of people trying to create successful local businesses, and wanted to point out the positives in a way that fitted with that. And you only have to look at Talalla to see that it is working. Just watching the way dogs bound over to make friends on the beach here, trusting you will be kind to them, is amazing. As the dogs look better, so the tourists love seeing them around, and so the business owners start to embrace them too. They treat them better, and the dogs become friendlier, and the whole cycle works really well.

In Arugam Bay, on the east coast, where we regularly head for CNVRs, there is an interesting divide. It is a real surfers' paradise, so the dogs there are getting completely spoilt by the tourists, and as such have become a bit racist! When we are trying to catch them to bring them in for vaccination and neutering, we have to send out the white volunteers to pick them up, and keep the Sri Lankan dog catchers back. But go down the road just a couple of miles where there is no tourism and the dogs have probably never seen a white person, and the reverse happens – the dogs will generally only let locals approach. It is interesting how the experiences they must go through in each area can influence their behaviour.

It is lovely to hear tourists who have been touring the island comment on the state of the dogs in Talalla and our area as being the happiest and healthiest they have come across. It is only a shame that the same cannot yet be said of dogs all over Sri Lanka. One day!

In terms of actually bringing a dog to us for treatment, I've got to be honest, it can be hit and miss with tourists.

It is important that people look at the dogs with a sense of the different culture, standards, priorities and requirements there are out here. You can't shoehorn Sri Lankan street dogs into the mould of how life is for UK dogs and expect it to work. A lot of this is about understanding street dogs and their lifestyles, but also about accepting what is possible.

If I am ever asked for help, but I don't think it is needed, I never just say no, but will always try and explain. So, for example, if someone calls to say Fido, a puppy on their beach, seems to be scratching a bit and might have fleas, and can we treat him, I explain just how pointless it would be. Flea treatment needs to be administered every month and we can't go around to see every dog in the area every month – or we would have no money or staff left for the actual serious issues.

I have learnt that dogs like Fido aren't a priority, as there are millions of dogs worse off, and quite frankly if some fleas are all he is dealing with, he is doing well! But I understand that it is tough, and they are right to check. Sending me a photo or describing his skin can ensure it is just a minor case of fleas as opposed to mange, in which case we would bring him in. I feel for the person who has called in, and want to support them in their helplessness, even if that is just a matter of educating them on why I said no.

These animals are not the same as dogs back home, where the main concerns are often if they get a fluffy enough bed, a pretty lead, and are walked two or three times a day. There is nothing wrong with dogs being treated in such a precious way, but it just doesn't translate over here. We need to keep the focus on helping these dogs with the basics such as freedom and, most crucially, health care.

Some of the time, concerned tourists are the absolute best. For example, someone might see a dog near their hotel every day and be concerned at a mass growing around its groin, and will research us on social media, then ring for advice. Other times they see an injured dog and actually bring them in, which is the ideal situation for us and our time-strapped staff. We had some absolute stars last year who diverted four hours off their planned holiday route and paid a driver a heap of cash to bring a dog to us when they saw her get hit by a car. Ella, as she was named – after the town where she was picked up – made a full recovery from the multiple fractures in her back legs, but wouldn't have survived without those kind-hearted people.

Of course not all dogs are easily scooped up, though, and then we really appreciate the call. At least, we appreciate it within reason. The person needs to either still have sight of the dog, or be able to give very specific instructions and information. For example, a lady recently emailed us photos of a dog whose state concerned her, and told us where on the beach she spotted him each day. As a creature of habit we stood a good chance of finding him, and it was in a village only ten kilometres away, so worth giving it a go. It was clear from the pictures that he had pretty chronic mange and was going to need some treatment to get it under control.

But other times it becomes more what I call 'guilt transference'. So we'll get a call: 'Hi, I was on the bus travelling to Galle, and saw a dog hit by a car.'

'Do you know which road you were on? Or the rough location? Do you know if the dog was badly injured?'

No. It turns out they just caught a glimpse out the window, and didn't really know where they were, oh and actually, it was two days ago. Ah. Even worse are those who email information about an accident that happened a week or so on, once they are home from their holiday.

We can't afford the time to send staff off on a wild-goose chase, to a town sixty kilometres away from the clinic, based on very little information that is now several days out of date. But the caller hangs up feeling relieved, the weight has been lifted because as far as they are concerned they have done their best. But then the guilt has been passed to me. I feel bad every time I say no to a call-out with such a minute chance of success, but we don't have unlimited time, finances, or staff resources to spend on a mission that probably has zero chance of success. It will play on my mind though. Is the dog now lying in a ditch in pain because we didn't go and find it? Is it about to die, when with my treatment it could survive?

I know of course that person wasn't calling to make me feel bad, but by passing on a vague sighting, they feel absolved of any guilt or responsibility, and it becomes an experience they once had in Sri Lanka. Whereas for me it is another time I have potentially failed a dog and I have to live with that thought.

In no way am I trying to discourage someone from getting in touch. Spotting an injured dog, caring enough to act on it, then finding our details, is more than 99 per cent of the population would do. I would just like people to take that little bit longer to gather the information that could make it a feasible rescue.

Other times, misplaced good intentions can actually see tourists causing more harm than good to a dog. Obviously, I love to see tourists befriend the local dogs, give time and affection to those they come across on their travels, and look out for their well-being where possible. But it needs to be within the confines of what is best for a Sri Lankan street dog.

Picture this: A couple are travelling through the country for a month and, a few days into their trip, come across a puppy at the side of the road in a village in the north of the island. Look how adorable he is! Surely a dog this young shouldn't be so near the road, what if a car were to hit him? And what could he possibly be eating? It doesn't take long for them to convince themselves that he is living a hellish life, and the kindest thing they can do is scoop up Pip (as they have decided to name him) and take him with them on their trip.

So, for the next three weeks Pip is petted, stroked, fed a bit of everything his new humans eat, and snuck into hotel rooms with the couple. This is the life!

Then suddenly it is the couple's last night, and they are down in Mirissa on the south coast taking their last photos of Pip for Instagram, with a sunset behind him. What a cute holiday accessory he has been . . .

They ask their guesthouse owner to take him on as a pet, and are told 'yes' because what else can they say? It feels as though it is part of the hospitality requirement for the guests. Then off the couple head on their flight, leaving Pip behind, confused, and now having to get used to yet another kind of life. Either the hotel owner will keep his word, given under pressure, and has a financial burden he didn't ask for, or he will turn Pip out to fend for himself.

Now Pip is two hundred and fifty miles from the only area he had known before, his mum will have given up the search for him, and he no longer has the company of his siblings. Dogs are territorial, and he will now need to fight to get a patch somewhere new. He might also have left a guardian behind in the north, so needs to find a new food source, and after three weeks sleeping in a bed, the ground feels hard to him. Occasionally a couple like this will contact us, but we are an animal hospital, not a shelter. We can direct them to local places where they could maybe take him, but unless the puppy is injured, we will not take him in. It is not part of our aim to take on healthy puppies to rehome.

But it is tough to say no, and I do have to take a deep breath and not go off on a lecture! I will always explain what would have been better, in the hope that they might behave differently if the situation comes up again.

So I guess what I want to say to any person who wants to take a puppy away from the situation they found it in, please don't, unless there is something actually wrong with it. Even then, get in touch with us, or any charity that might be nearer – for example, Embark if you are in Colombo. Like so much else, when visiting another country, people need to learn to look at the situation with some local knowledge, and not just judge it with a western mindset.

The reality is, this is unintentionally irresponsible behaviour that is not helpful to the dog in the slightest. It is literally the opposite of responsible tourism or responsible animal care. And yet we see it so, so much. People believe they love that animal for those two weeks, but they fail to think of its long-term well-being. Think ahead, beyond your holiday, to what that dog needs, and leave it where it is.

This is not meant to sound harsh as I realise they want to help, but they have just gone about it in completely the wrong way. They are leaving others to pick up the mess and leaving the dog in a vulnerable position when they were quite safe where they were in the first place.

I am learning something new here every day. Five years on, my take on everything in this country is still changing and evolving, so of course tourists won't have a complete handle on it three days into their trip. But if they really want to make a difference, leave that dog with its mum, take the time to understand the overall situation, and get involved with WECare, or one of the other charities doing amazing work.

The majority of tourists are so well intentioned really, and once we explain the situation of how things work, both in the country and in our clinic, they understand, and embrace what they have learnt. Lots of people leave us donations, either when spotting one of our charity boxes, talking to one of our volunteers on the beach, or once they have returned to the UK, and have researched the island's dogs.

We are looking at ways to tackle these problems in the long run and educate tourists. The fact that so many of them want to help is great, it is just harnessing that in the right way, and making sure their expectations of the country's dogs are realistic.

While we don't have the resources right now to do regular tours of the clinic, when people have called and asked to visit, and things aren't too hectic (once in a blue moon), then we have given them the tour of everything that goes on, in exchange for a donation to the charity, ending with a great play session with our garden dogs. I think that can be really eye-opening and educational for people when they see the challenges we are facing.

Then we have started doing things such as coffee mornings at Talalla Retreat, to talk to their visitors about what we do and how they can help. And we would love to get some articles in in-flight magazines on responsible tourism, and in the press generally. Tourist education is just as important as local education for me, especially with the tourism boom happening at the moment. The more tools I can give people to work with, to make sure the dogs have the best lives, the better.

People often ask us about adopting a dog from Sri Lanka and taking them back to their own country, but I don't generally agree with overseas adoptions.

There are problems with stray or unwanted dogs wherever you are in the world, so why not help those first? If you really want to help a dog, then do so locally.

If you are in the UK, they are being put to sleep in places like Battersea Dogs' Home on a weekly basis, so if you like the idea of actually saving a life when you get a dog as opposed to going to breeders, then that is exactly what you will be doing by going there. This idea that it might somehow be more exotic to get a dog from abroad needs to stop.

These dogs are Sri Lanka's responsibility, and just moving them on doesn't feel like the solution. That the dogs should be helped within their own country and own environment is something I feel very strongly about.

It is worth remembering too that these dogs have been on the streets for years, and as such their breed has evolved to cope with that. They are used to their freedom and a lot of socialising with other dogs, so to take them to a UK climate, where they may be the owners' only dog, and kept in the house for much of the day, won't sit well with them.

Even getting them there shouldn't be undertaken lightly. It can be hugely stressful for the dog, travelling halfway around the world, going through all sorts of checks, potentially being quarantined, and then being rehomed in a country so completely different to the one he has lived in so far. It is also a costly process.

We had one lady here for a while who had a good insight into how we worked, or so I thought. Then after she left she emailed to ask about exporting a couple of the dogs for adoption to Canada.

I told her I didn't normally recommend it, but as I knew she was experienced with dogs if she wanted to push ahead, we could talk further, but I warned her it would cost around $5,000 a dog for everything she would need to do.

She said that money was no problem, but as the conversation carried on it turned out the dogs weren't actually for her, but were to go to Canada to be put into the care of another adoption agency where they could then be adopted by local people. What? I don't even understand why you would do that. Is it that people like the idea of having a more 'exotic' dog? There is no way I was going to put any of our dogs into a scheme that would see them travelling halfway around the world with no definite home to go to.

Besides, if you have $10,000 going spare, the difference that could make to many dogs' lives over here, as opposed to just moving two, is huge. I suggested as much, but I never heard from her again.

Taking on a dog in need on your own doorstep really is the best choice you can make.

CHAPTER TWENTY-EIGHT

A COUNTRY UNDER ATTACK

On 21 April 2019, Easter Sunday, I got a rare morning off and decided to escape down to the beach for a surf. Just before I headed into the water, I got a message from a friend in India.

Janey! Are you okay?

Yep, all good, thanks, you? I typed quickly, thinking it was just a casual check in.

Grabbing my board I headed into the sea for a few hours.

By the time I was back out again, it was like all hell had broken loose. My phone was going crazy with message notifications and the few people on the beach were walking around in a kind of daze.

I read through my messages and tried to get to grips with what was happening. There had been a set of terrorist bombings, mostly around Colombo, and one on the east coast. It made no sense. Who? Why?

Three churches and three high-end hotels had been targeted by suicide bombers. I had been in one of them, the Shangri-La, for dinner with mates just thirty-six hours before, sat in the same restaurant where these poor people had lost their lives. These sorts of people didn't care who they killed, it was indiscriminate madness.

I tried to get hold of friends in those areas, while trying to process the awfulness of it all. This was not something I had envisaged the country facing.

The places where the bombs exploded made it seem like it was westerners and Christians that were being targeted but it didn't add up. There was no animosity between those groups and the rest of the people on the island, and the country was starting to thrive, in part because of tourism. Why would someone want to destroy that growing relationship now?

Details kept changing, but eventually the death toll was confirmed as 258, with another 500 people injured. I couldn't believe it, and just felt so confused. If you had told me the country was going to face a disaster, and asked me what it would be, I'd have guessed something caused by nature, like another tsunami, or an earthquake. But this? A man-made disaster, where a group of people had actually chosen the path of destruction? Horrendous and nonsensical.

In the following days the government announced a state of national emergency. There was a social media shutdown – something I fully agreed with because of the amount of misinformation getting spread, as well as the risk of people attempting to use it to coordinate further attacks or retaliation.

There was also a curfew, a ban on face coverings including burqas and niqabs, and an announcement of an investigation into what had happened, but people were confused and struggling to trust the authorities.

As word emerged that those responsible had ties to the Islamic State terrorists, there was a spate of retaliation attacks against random innocent Muslims – vandalism, shops ransacked, people beaten up, a kind of mob rule. Luckily, reports implied there was no real organisation to them, and nothing happened in our region.

I was worried that it was opening up past tensions between Muslims and Buddhists, and that these attacks would hand people an excuse to let off steam and resort to their prejudices. There was a defeatist air of 'here we go again', and a risk that the country would slide backwards and people would get drawn into the arguments of old.

I chatted to some of the local Buddhist lads to try and gauge the mood, and they reassured me: 'Don't worry, we aren't about to do anything. We have Muslim friends and know that a few bad people don't represent them all.' It was good to hear. The sooner peace could be restored, the better.

All of this of course had an effect on WECare. A couple of volunteers due to fly out to join us on the day after the attacks understandably pulled out, and then others followed suit. It wasn't just people worrying for their own safety but there were other key factors, such as insurance companies refusing to give out policies to travellers, while the British government were advising against all but essential travel to the region.

The locals were afraid too. The UK is known for its stoic attitude in the face of the various attacks suffered there – people purposefully taking the tube after the 7 July 2005 bombing, or making a conscious decision to walk across London Bridge after the 2017 attack – anything to show that they wouldn't be cowed by the terrorists, and they had failed in their efforts. The same cannot be said for the Sri Lankans as they didn't have that same faith that the government were acting behind the scenes to ensure their safety. There was incredibly concerning news emerging that the government had been given a warning of these attacks three times, and failed to act on it, so everyone was afraid to leave their homes in case there were more to come. Coffee shops stood empty, normally busy shopping areas were deserted. It made me so angry – Sri Lankans have struggled enough over the years. Could they not just have some luck, and be allowed to build a successful, happy country?

People had lost family, homes and livelihoods, and I was worried the country was going to slide back into a civil war.

The long-term effect on the economy of the island worried me, for the sake of the Sri Lankans. So many of them had become dependent on tourism for a living, and this fell away instantly. The beaches that had been buzzing just weeks before were now empty, hotels found all their bookings had been cancelled, and the airport was eerily quiet. But while this meant many of the locals might be left in a desperate state, I got angry with friends with businesses in the capital who began talking of packing up and going home for the same reasons. It wasn't life changing on the same level for them. If you have chosen to move here and make a life on the island, isn't it right that you ride through the rough with the Sri Lankans, as well as the smooth? I felt like it was more important than ever that we pulled together and proved that we were part of the community. I did my best through social media and chatting to people to prove that it was business as normal in the country, and people should not be deterred from visiting one of the most incredible places on this earth.

Thankfully, things slowly began to pick up again. Lots of the extra security measures were kept in place, but (touch wood) nothing further has happened since then, in the run-up to writing this book. With any luck it was a horrific one-off attack.

Neighbours pulled together and helped each other out, travel advice began to relax, and slowly but surely the cafés and shops started to fill with locals and visitors again.

It will definitely take time to get the country fully back on its feet, and it has shaken people and shown them – once again – how easily their livelihoods can be taken away. But the recovery is well under way.

At the time seventy people were arrested in connection with the bombings, but no one has actually been found to have been responsible for them. I think the correct people being found guilty and held accountable for those horrific events will really prove to Sri Lankans that things are getting back on track, and that is the least they deserve.

• CHAPTER TWENTY-NINE •

FILM CREW ROLL INTO TOWN

An email landed in my inbox from a TV producer, asking if he could come and make a documentary about WECare. It was an instant dilemma. The last thing I wanted to do was put the charity in jeopardy by putting us on an international stage for people to pick holes in us again. But I also knew just how beneficial the BBC documentary had been to us financially.

On a personal level I was also a bit nervous of opening myself up to criticism again. Was it a good idea to keep cruising along under the radar, or should we be promoting ourselves more?

In the end I knew if we could raise a similar figure off the back of it as we had last time, it would be absolutely incredible for the charity. Even though I hadn't shared my worries with the rest of the team, the WECare funds were running low. Like, seriously low. Low enough that I honestly didn't know how I was going to be able to cover rent, salaries, dog food and medication for the next six months. I was feeling immensely guilty about the salary I'd begun paying myself just a few months before, and had wondered if I should be stopping it again.

The tipping point came when I discovered it was for a documentary series for Channel 5 called *New Lives in the Wild*, fronted by Ben Fogle. With a presenter like him at the helm, I was sure he would give a true representation of us – and that the programme would have a broad reach. I figured I would be crazy not to say yes.

Fast forward a few months, and Ben arrived, along with the camera crew, who did a great job of fitting in, and were fun to have around.

Ben came across as a nice guy who clearly loved dogs and was at home with talking all things medical – in part, I guess, thanks to his dad, who is a vet. The poor guy seemed tired, as the crew had been filming all over the world before Sri Lanka, and he was missing his family, but it didn't stop him making a real effort and throwing himself into the daily experience alongside us.

We had made all the Sri Lankan footage for the BBC documentary ourselves, so it was good for an outside crew to be responsible for content this time, especially as it was for a one-hour slot, so there was potential to include much more. I didn't get a say on content as such, but I was able to voice any concerns I had, and the production team were clear they were supportive of our work. They made me feel really comfortable, and I was able to put my trust in them.

I was filmed in the clinic handling typical cases as they came in, out in the tuk-tuk dealing with street dogs, at a CNVR, in my own home, and sat chatting to Ben about the changes in my life.

It was interesting to see Ben's mindset shift over the week. I think he wasn't sure quite what the hell we were doing when he first arrived – why I wasn't getting angry at locals, why we were returning dogs to the street, and whether we were making a difference.

But as the week went on and he saw the challenges we faced, he began to understand. I think there were a couple of key moments for him. Seeing the owned dog that was brought in with an ear absolutely teeming with maggots, and me explaining this was normal. I got on with pulling hundreds of them out of the pockets of flesh they were hiding in, which was a real shock to him. He kept saying, 'This is unbelievable, I've never seen anything as horrific as that. The dog would be taken away from its owner if this was in the UK. It's heartbreaking.'

Then the other turning point was coming out on one of our CNVR days. He got involved trying to catch some of the dogs in nets (he gave it a good go, but sorry, Ben, I'll not be offering you a job doing it any time soon!) and saw the endless flow of dogs, and the number we were able to treat in a day.

By the end of the week he said he thought I needed to step back sometimes and take a breather, but that I made a great role model and he was pleased there were people like me for his daughter to look up to. It was a lovely thing to hear.

There was a gap of seven months before the show was released, which gave me far too much time to think. I was really nervous about how the publicity would affect the charity, but I was also watching our funds dripping away, and praying it would get on air as soon as possible, in the hope we would get some donations.

By the time we were given the release date, 7 May 2019, I had prepared myself. I was hopeful that I had a thicker skin, but I still vowed that I wouldn't read any of the online comments, and I was due back to the UK for a work visit soon after, so my support network was at the ready!

The worst bit, though, was that we couldn't watch it at the same time as everyone else, as it wasn't airing in Sri Lanka, so I had to wait and watch social media to see how it was received.

I sat there in front of my computer like a nervous wreck as nine p.m. UK time (one-thirty a.m. our time) approached. The first messages that came through were positive, from friends and supporters of the charity who knew it was on, but it was when the new people began appearing that my heart was in my mouth waiting to see what they would say …

Suddenly it went nuts! Other team members were manning social media too, but even then we got absolutely swamped. But thank bloody goodness, everyone was so lovely and positive, and supportive. If I'd had time to actually stop and think about what was being said I'd have been utterly overwhelmed, but as it was I just had to keep bashing out responses, as I wanted to reply to everyone who made the effort to find us.

Lots of people were asking about donating, how they could volunteer, what equipment they could send. The one frustrating thing is our website went down and I was worried some great offers wouldn't get through, so I turned all my attention to trying to get that back up and running. Between trying to fix that, and the messages that just kept coming, I'm not sure I even got to sleep that night, and we started working the social media in shifts.

But in the first few weeks a staggering £60,000 was donated.

We also got some good coverage in the press, although I was mortified when the *Mail Online* focused in on my love life – or lack of! – when I joked on the show about being left on the shelf. I was disappointed that they chose that angle, as it felt like we had achieved so much with WECare, but they had gone down the unfortunate media route of picking a problem in a female doing a good thing.

The article focused on the one area in my life that hasn't worked so well, and the message was like, 'Well, she's done all this, but because she hasn't got a man, she's not really a success.'

Then one of my biggest dreams of the last couple of years came true. A lovely gentleman, who had watched the show, got in touch and offered to buy us X-ray and ultrasound machines. Not just contribute towards one, but actually cover the cost of both pieces of equipment outright. It was crazy and I couldn't quite believe it was happening, so didn't tell the others until the money had actually landed in the account, in case I raised their hopes and it fell through. Then the cash arrived and, well, I cried! It was great to tell the team the best news, and the donor can be so sure how grateful we are, for what a huge difference he has made to the lives of so many dogs.

We ordered the machines and added them to a container, along with lots of other much-needed equipment that had been donated, or paid for with donations.

Then we kitted out one of the consultation rooms in the clinic with lead proofing, and everything needed for radiation safety, and we were good to go.

To say it has made a huge difference to the treatment we are able to offer the dogs is an understatement.

• CHAPTER THIRTY •

LONG MAY THE ROLLERCOASTER CONTINUE

No one volunteers at WECare for an easy ride or for the money – everyone is driven by the love of dogs, and can end up working all hours. But in a rare one-off, Jo went home mid-afternoon one day. Calamity George had been hanging around near the clinic and, spotting Jo leave, decided to accompany her home. As they got to the road outside their house, he started scrapping with another dog. They often sort things out between themselves, but this was escalating and getting a bit nasty, so Jo went to try and split them up, when a tuk-tuk came flying down the road. The driver made no attempt to avoid the group, and hit George right in front of Jo, and drove on.

The first I knew of it was when a hysterical Jo called me, crying, 'Can you come now!'

I jumped in a tuk-tuk with Chaz. A bit of me was worried, but I also knew that this was George, our total little trouper who had survived just about everything nature could throw at him. He was the dog you would see wandering around the village and think, 'Oh god, George, get out of the road!' But he would always move in time. A cat and its nine lives had nothing on George. Therefore I was sure a little knock from a tuk-tuk wasn't going to affect him.

By the time we arrived George was up in the flat, lying on a cushion with a bad wound on his back leg and seemed, unsurprisingly, to be in shock. Jo was covered in blood and sobbing her eyes out. Jo is one of our tougher cookies and you don't see emotion getting the better of her very often, so it was horrible to see her like that.

'He'll be all right,' I tried to reassure her and, whipping George up in my arms, took him back to the clinic in the tuk-tuk. Everyone was freaking out when we arrived as the whole clinic loves George, and knows what an amazing dog he is. But as I got into the prep room I needed space to work and tried to direct them towards supporting Jo, who was out in the garden with the dogs. I genuinely thought George was going to be okay.

It was all hands on deck as it was a trauma situation, and we were all working to get shock-rate fluids into him, give him pain relief, get him warm, and manage everything, while assessing the damage. But before I could do anything, George crashed. I couldn't believe it. My stomach dropped, it was the most hideous feeling. I started doing CPR. Were there worse injuries internally that I hadn't had a moment to discover, or was the shock too much for his poor body? I could feel everyone's eyes on me knowing I was the only one who might be able to save him. The room was totally silent as everyone stood there watching me pumping at George's chest, willing me to succeed. Lisa and Amy, two other staff members who lived with Jo, were watching through the glass window. The pressure was palpable and I tried everything I could think of, but it didn't work, we had lost him.

I went outside to tell Jo, and she, Amy, Lisa and I collapsed together in tears. I tried to console Jo, but I was devastated too. He had been one of the clinic dogs for two years before moving in with Jo, and we all felt like we had lost a best friend. It was just so traumatic, and shit, and too, too sad.

We buried our George outside the office, alongside Ticky, the two of them forever close.

I know his death absolutely broke Jo's heart, but in her typical style she put a brave face on and cracked on with life, focusing on the rest of our dogs. George and Jo suited each other perfectly – both absolute troopers.

One of the guys pulled together a video of George's best moments that had been caught on camera, and that cheered some people up, but I found it too sad to watch. As usual, I kept wondering if there was anything I could have done differently.

George was so well known around the village that a lot of people were both angry and sad about his death, including Jo's landlord Dinush and his family who had become so attached to him. Dinush, who had been so wary of dogs at the start, was genuinely heartbroken, and went around looking at all the tuk-tuks to see if any had a George-shaped dent, determined that someone should be held accountable for such reckless driving.

Out of the other two dogs in the house, singing Baz has always been really independent anyway, and didn't seem too affected by George's departure. But Lucy, who we think actually saw the accident as it happened, refused to leave the house for a good while after.

Caring Dinush did what he could to help cheer her up, even bringing around huge bowls of curry for the dogs – a prawn one for Lucy and chicken for Baz, because, you know, they both obviously have their preferences!

Unfortunately, it is a perfect example of what I mean about

things being another level out here. At home, losing your dog is horrendous, but it is very unlikely that you would see them run over in front of you, then see their chest pumped while they died in front of you, and know that the whole thing was caused by some idiot having no regard for a dog's life. It is so full-on.

But in the typical highs and lows of Sri Lanka, straight after bad news for one dog, there is often good news for another – or in this case, two of them.

My beloved tripods Bonnie and Lucky, who I had accepted were pretty much going to be WECare residents for life, found homes. And not just any old homes, but the best homes ever, just two hundred metres away from each other, so they can still hang out and play together! I was so happy.

Jo had gone on a real mission to get them homes, and prove that despite missing a leg, they more than made up for it in character, spirit, and affection. Both of them had been nearly adopted twice previously, but the plans had then fallen through last minute, so she was adamant that this time it would work.

We went back to check up on the two of them a week or so after they went off with their new families, and I couldn't have been happier with what I saw.

All twelve members of Lucky's new human family and her new Pomeranian sister were there to meet us when we arrived, and excitedly told us all about her adventures. Then Bonnie's family told us that each morning Bonnie got egg and chicken, along with a cup of tea. I laughed my head off, but loved it, as it showed just how much she was a part of the family. It was also clear from their home that they weren't well off, but the fact they were putting that care into Bonnie warmed my heart.

The biggest sign of all was that although both dogs were really pleased to see us, they didn't try and follow when we left, but stayed with their new families, clearly already content that this is where they wanted to be.

A happy ending for those two just made my month.

It is still an absolute rollercoaster, every single day. At times it feels we are clinging on by our absolute fingertips, and everything could fall apart with a simple nudge. We have no security. Our building is only leased, and although we have put so much money into the place, and adapted it to be our own perfect little surgery, in theory we could be made to leave at any point. Recently I was told that one of the temples was looking to take over nearby land and, if they did, they wanted us gone. It was a reminder, yet again, of how vulnerable we are, and that five years' work could be ended if someone more powerful wanted to get rid of us. The only solution is to one day own a clinic of our own.

I have a lot of dreams for the future. As well as owning our own clinic, I'd like more equipment so that we can treat the dogs with greater accuracy and efficiency, as well as another vet who wants to stay in Sri Lanka working for WECare permanently.

On a larger scale, I would like to expand across Sri Lanka, and perhaps open clinics in other parts of Asia and Africa where there are street dog populations in need of someone to care for them.

They are big dreams, I know. But I know too that what we have already achieved would have got me laughed out of a room before I'd set off on this adventure.

Will I always be the crazy dog lady of Sri Lanka? Who knows. Sometimes I think heading back to the UK, taking on a simple job and having a family, has its appeal. Other times I think I'd like to move to another country and start a fresh adventure. But I know deep down that unless I can stand here with my hand on my heart and say the dogs won't suffer for my absence, I'll never leave them.

I honestly think I was put on this earth for the purpose of

helping these dogs, so I am going to fulfil that. I've got a dedicated and driven team around me, and we aren't about to give up, whatever difficulties come our way.

People are always saying what we are doing is selfless, but it's not – if anything it is selfish, as we love what we do every day, and the time we get to spend with the animals. In reality, I get as much back from these amazing dogs as I give them, if not more. Anyone who has ever properly loved a dog will know what I mean. Just make sure, wherever you are in the world, you always do right by these beautiful creatures.

To find out more about
WECare Worldwide and Janey, check out:

www.wecareworldwide.org.uk

Follow WECare Worldwide on social media at:
Facebook: WECareWorldwide
Twitter: @WECare-SriLanka
Instagram: @wecare_srilanka

And if you want to donate any spare
pennies to the fabulous cause, visit:
gofundme.com/wecarevethospital